# Borders, Frames and Decorative Motifs

from the
1862 Derriey Typographic Catalog

# Borders, Frames and Decorative Motifs

from the
1862 Derriey Typographic Catalog

BY CHARLES DERRIEY

Dover Publications, Inc., New York

Copyright © 1987 by Dover Publications, Inc.
All rights reserved under Pan American and International Copyright Conventions.

Published in Canada by General Publishing Company, Ltd., 30 Lesmill Road, Don Mills, Toronto, Ontario.
Published in the United Kingdom by Constable and Company, Ltd., 10 Orange Street, London WC2H 7EG.

*Borders, Frames and Decorative Motifs from the 1862 Derriey Typographic Catalog*, first published by Dover Publications, Inc., in 1987, is a new selection of 113 plates from *Spécimen-Album*, a portfolio originally published by the Gravure et Fonderie de Charles Derriey, Paris, in 1862. The plates on pages 110–113, printed in brown ink in the original edition, are here reproduced in black. The Publisher's Note and Contents have been prepared specially for the present edition.

DOVER *Pictorial Archive* SERIES

Manufactured in the United States of America
Dover Publications, Inc., 31 East 2nd Street, Mineola, N.Y. 11501

**Library of Congress Cataloging-in-Publication Data**

Derriey, Charles.
  Borders, frames and decorative motifs from the 1862 Derriey typographic catalog.

  (Dover pictorial archive series)
  "A new selection of 113 plates from Spécimen-album, a portfolio originally published by the Gravure et fonderie de Charles Derriey, Paris, in 1862"—Verso t.p.
  1. Printers' ornaments.  2. Type ornaments.  3. Borders, Ornamental (Decorative arts)  I. Gravure et fonderie de Charles Derriey. Spécimen-album.  II. Title.  III. Series.
Z250.3.D47   1987      686.2'24              86-29181
ISBN 0-486-25322-8 (pbk.)

# PUBLISHER'S NOTE

The first half of the nineteenth century witnessed the transformation of printing from a purely manual craft into a semi-mechanical industry. Two inventions—the printing machine and the paper-making machine—made it possible to produce printed matter more quickly and more economically than was previously possible. The effects of the Industrial Revolution on printing, however, were far from just mechanical in nature. Perhaps of equal significance was the accompanying dramatic increase in the market for the printing industry's wares and the consequent marked effect on typography and design.

The tremendous technological advances that enabled manufacturers to produce goods more economically also allowed the middle and lower classes to purchase a greater number of products. At the same time, the population of the Western world was rising at an incredible rate, nearly doubling in the years between 1800 and 1850. Together these two factors gave rise to an ever-increasing demand for consumer goods, which subsequently led to a rapid expansion in the production of such goods. The resulting increased flow of merchandise into the marketplace created growing commercial competition, giving rise to a need for more effective and creative product merchandising. The printing industry was called upon to provide trade and consumer advertisements aimed at new and larger markets, as well as business cards, tickets, letterheads, invoices, banknotes, book covers, title pages, programs, certificates and so on. This increased demand on printers in turn led to an increased demand on typefounders for new display types and ornamentation suitable for use in advertising and jobbing work. Typefounding establishments responded with a copious production of new material, so that, whereas only a few decades earlier a very small range of typographic display material was available to printers, by 1860 the choice of types and ornamental designs was large and quite diverse.

It is not surprising that the same spirit of lavish eclecticism that marked the Victorian age in general also prevailed in the design of new types and ornamentation. The period prior to 1890, when more austere fashions set in, saw typefounders ply their trade with a very free creative rein. They drew upon the entire Western heritage of typographic styles, supplemented their designs with intricate ornamentation, often of Eastern origin, and combined the motifs in novel ways. In addition, the Victorians' lust for decoration and embellishment pervaded the industry. Fantastic letter forms; exquisitely detailed frames, borders and vignettes; and elegantly graceful calligraphic flourishes were combined in typical high Victorian style to adorn printed matter of nearly every variety.

By some later standards of design, many typographical practices of the Victorian era would be considered extreme. (For instance, it was quite common and proper at that time to include as many different typefaces as possible in one publication—even on one page.) However, today more than ever, the ornamental designs created by Victorian typefounders are sought after by artists, designers and craftspeople. Though perhaps not as artistically innovative as design motifs from other eras, nor as uniformly directed in an aesthetic sense as some, for sheer versatility, ornate beauty and sumptuousness, Victorian-era typographic designs have few peers, as is evidenced by the present volume of display material.

This superb collection is a reproduction of 113 single-color plates from *Spécimen-Album*, an unbound portfolio originally issued in 1862 as a catalog of typographic design specimens by the Parisian foundry of Charles Derriey. The deluxe presentation of typographic specimen books published by the trade was not unusual in the nineteenth century. Not only did they serve as catalogs of the foundry's stock, but also as examples of artistically executed applications of the type forms and ornamentation offered. Derriey's 1862 catalog was no exception. It offered for sale to printing jobbers a tremendous assortment of display types and printer's ornaments: vignettes (dingbats, headpieces, tailpieces, etc.), rules, flourishes, corner elements and much more, including a selection of Victorian frames and border material as diverse as you are ever likely to see. The last portion of the catalog was devoted to sample compositions that illustrate the graphic possibilities of Derriey's designs. For quick reference, a complete listing of the kinds of design elements and sample compositions available in this volume follows this Note in the Contents. Large borders, though not listed in the Contents, appear on every page. Omitted from the present selection were the color pages, music pages, sheets of ordinary straight rules and a few other pages of little typographic or design interest.

Recall, if you will, as you look through this book, that the purpose in 1862 of this volume's every image, either singly or in conjunction with other elements, was to enhance a project, be it an advertisement, notice or some business-related form. The same is true today. Yet, beyond this collection's obvious utility as a copyright-free "swipe-file," students of design will appreciate the broad survey of Victorian ornamentation contained in its pages, totally authentic not only in its elements, but also in the ensemble. And everyone with an eye for fanciful, distinctive and handsome design will simply enjoy browsing through this magnificent collection.

# CONTENTS

# Borders, Frames and Decorative Motifs

from the
1862 Derriey Typographic Catalog

# VIGNETTES

Gravure et Fonderie de CH. DERRIEY, PARIS, rue Notre-Dame-des-Champs, 6 et 12.

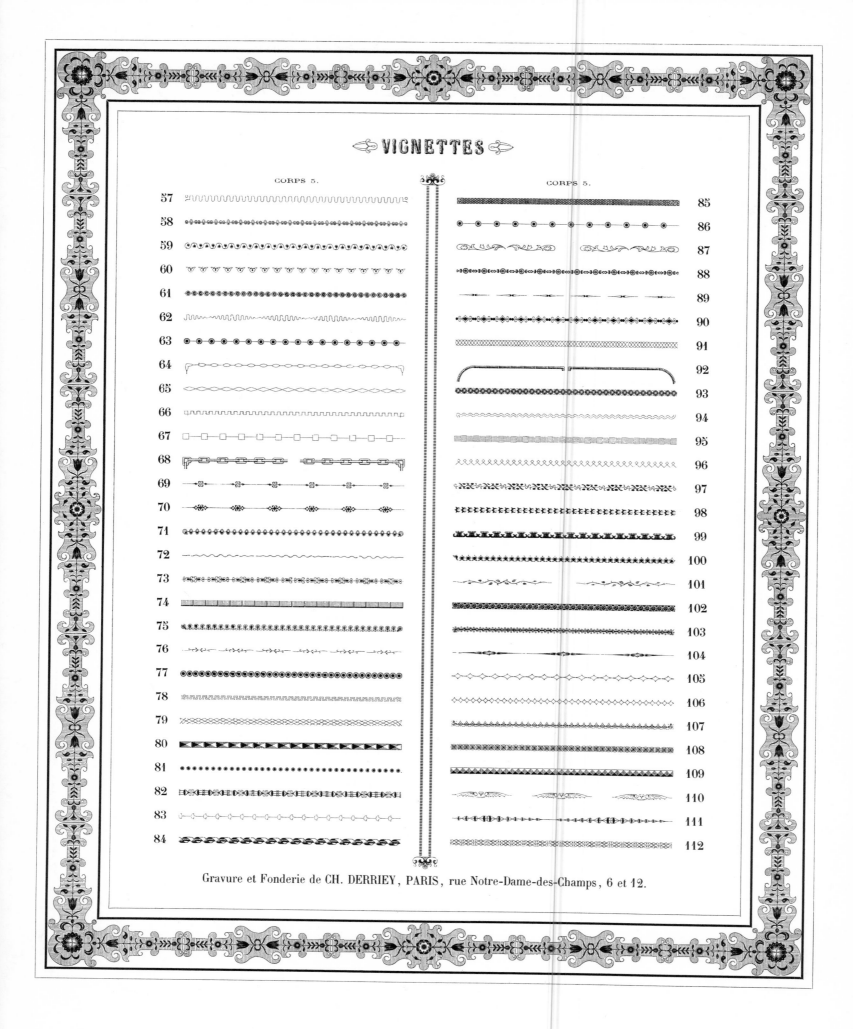

VIGNETTES

**CORPS 5.**

113 ~~~~~~~~~~~~~~~~~~~~~~~~~~~~~~~~~~~~
114 ~~~~~~~~~~~~~~~~~~~~~~~~~~~~~~~~~~~~
115 ~~~~~~~~~~~~~~~~~~~~~~~~~~~~~~~~~~~~
116 ●●●●●●●●●●●●●●●●●●●●●●●●●●●●●●●●●●●●●●
117 ~~~~~~~~~~~~~~~~~~~~~~~~~~~~~~~~~~~~
118 ~~~~~~~~~~~~~~~~~~~~~~~~~~~~~~~~~~~~
119 ~~~~~~~~~~~~~~~~~~~~~~~~~~~~~~~~~~~~
120 ~~~~~~~~~~~~~~~~~~~~~~~~~~~~~~~~~~~~
121 ←←←←←←←←←←←←←←←←←←←←←←←←←←←←←←←←→
122 ────────────────────────────────────
123 ~~~~~~~~~~~~~~~~~~~~~~~~~~~~~~~~~~~~
124 ~~~~~~~~~~~~~~~~~~~~~~~~~~~~~~~~~~~~
125 ~~~~~~~~~~~~~~~~~~~~~~~~~~~~~~~~~~~~
126 ~~~~~~~~~~~~~~~~~~~~~~~~~~~~~~~~~~~~
127 ════════════════════════════════════

**CORPS 10.**

128 ~~~~~~~~~~~~~~~~~~~~~~~~~~~~~~~~~~~~
129 ~~~~~~~~~~~~~~~~~~~~~~~~~~~~~~~~~~~~
130 ~~~~~~~~~~~~~~~~~~~~~~~~~~~~~~~~~~~~
131 ◇◇◇◇◇◇◇◇◇◇◇◇◇◇◇◇◇◇◇◇◇◇◇◇◇◇◇◇◇◇◇◇
132 ~~~~~~~~~~~~~~~~~~~~~~~~~~~~~~~~~~~~
133 ~~~~~~~~~~~~~~~~~~~~~~~~~~~~~~~~~~~~
134 ~~~~~~~~~~~~~~~~~~~~~~~~~~~~~~~~~~~~
135 ~~~~~~~~~~~~~~~~~~~~~~~~~~~~~~~~~~~~
136 ~~~~~~~~~~~~~~~~~~~~~~~~~~~~~~~~~~~~

**CORPS 10.**

137 ~~~~~~~~~~~~~~~~~~~~~~~~~~~~~~~~~~~~
138 ~~~~~~~~~~~~~~~~~~~~~~~~~~~~~~~~~~~~
139 ~~~~~~~~~~~~~~~~~~~~~~~~~~~~~~~~~~~~
140 ~~~~~~~~~~~~~~~~~~~~~~~~~~~~~~~~~~~~
141 ~~~~~~~~~~~~~~~~~~~~~~~~~~~~~~~~~~~~
142 ~~~~~~~~~~~~~~~~~~~~~~~~~~~~~~~~~~~~
143 ~~~~~~~~~~~~~~~~~~~~~~~~~~~~~~~~~~~~
144 ~~~~~~~~~~~~~~~~~~~~~~~~~~~~~~~~~~~~
145 ~~~~~~~~~~~~~~~~~~~~~~~~~~~~~~~~~~~~
146 ~~~~~~~~~~~~~~~~~~~~~~~~~~~~~~~~~~~~
147 ~~~~~~~~~~~~~~~~~~~~~~~~~~~~~~~~~~~~
148 ~~~~~~~~~~~~~~~~~~~~~~~~~~~~~~~~~~~~
149 ~~~~~~~~~~~~~~~~~~~~~~~~~~~~~~~~~~~~
150 ~~~~~~~~~~~~~~~~~~~~~~~~~~~~~~~~~~~~
151 ~~~~~~~~~~~~~~~~~~~~~~~~~~~~~~~~~~~~
152 ~~~~~~~~~~~~~~~~~~~~~~~~~~~~~~~~~~~~
153 ~~~~~~~~~~~~~~~~~~~~~~~~~~~~~~~~~~~~
154 ~~~~~~~~~~~~~~~~~~~~~~~~~~~~~~~~~~~~
155 ~~~~~~~~~~~~~~~~~~~~~~~~~~~~~~~~~~~~
156 ~~~~~~~~~~~~~~~~~~~~~~~~~~~~~~~~~~~~
157 ~~~~~~~~~~~~~~~~~~~~~~~~~~~~~~~~~~~~
158 ~~~~~~~~~~~~~~~~~~~~~~~~~~~~~~~~~~~~

*Gravure et Fonderie de CH. DERRIEY, PARIS, rue Notre-Dame-des-Champs, 6 et 12.*

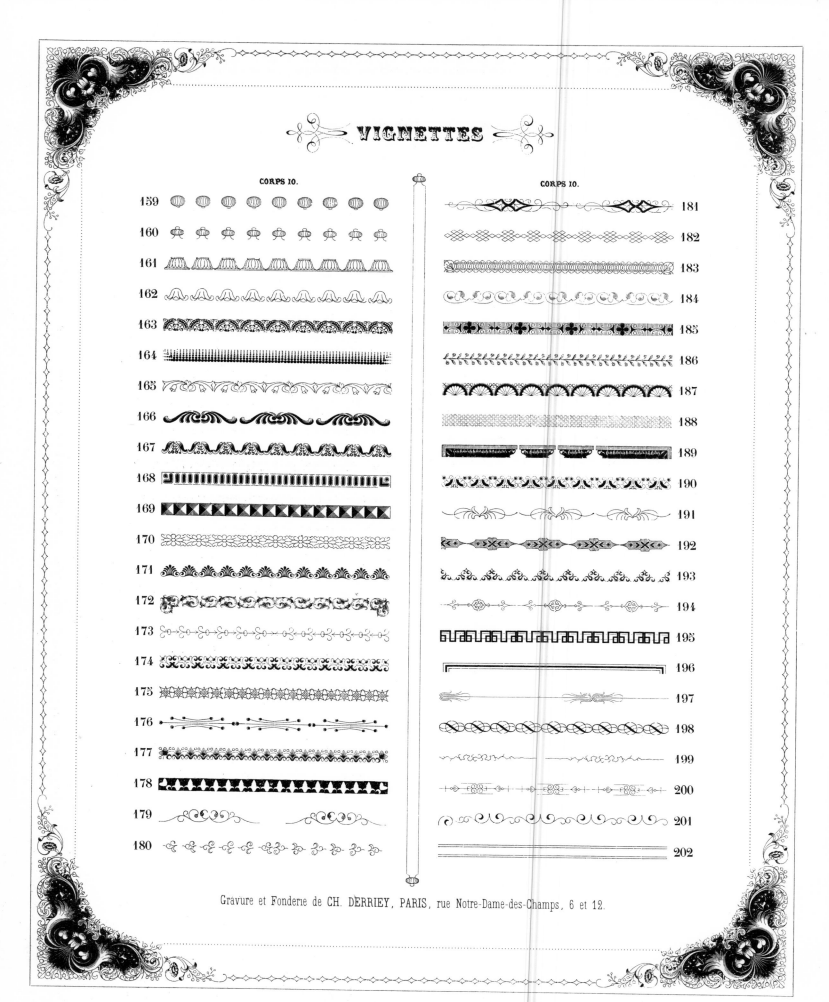

# VIGNETTES

CORPS 10.

CORPS 10.

Gravure et Fonderie de CH. DERRIEY, PARIS, rue Notre-Dame-des-Champs, 6 et 12.

# VIGNETTES

CORPS 10.

CORPS 10.

203
204
205
206
207
208
209
210
211
212
213
214
215
216
217
218
219
220
221
222
223
224

225
226
227
228
229
230
231
232
233
234
235
236
237
238
239
240
241
242
243
244
245
246

Gravure et Fonderie de CH. DERRIEY, PARIS, rue Notre-Dame-des-Champs, 6 et 12.

# VIGNETTES

CORPS 10.

CORPS 10.

247    269
248    270
249    271
250    272
251    273
252    274
253    275
254    276
255    277
256    278
257    279
258    280
259    281
260    282
261    283
262    284
263    285
264    286
265    287
266    288
267    289
268    290

Gravure et Fonderie de CH. DERRIEY, PARIS, rue Notre-Dame-des-Champs, 6 et 12.

# VIGNETTES

## CORPS 10.

291
292
293
294
295
296
297

## CORPS 15.

298
299
300
301
302
303
304
305
306
307
308

## CORPS 15.

309
310
311
312
313
314
315
316
317
318
319
320
321
322
323
324
325
326

Gravure et Fonderie de CH. DERRIEY, PARIS, rue Notre-Dame-des-Champs, 6 et 12.

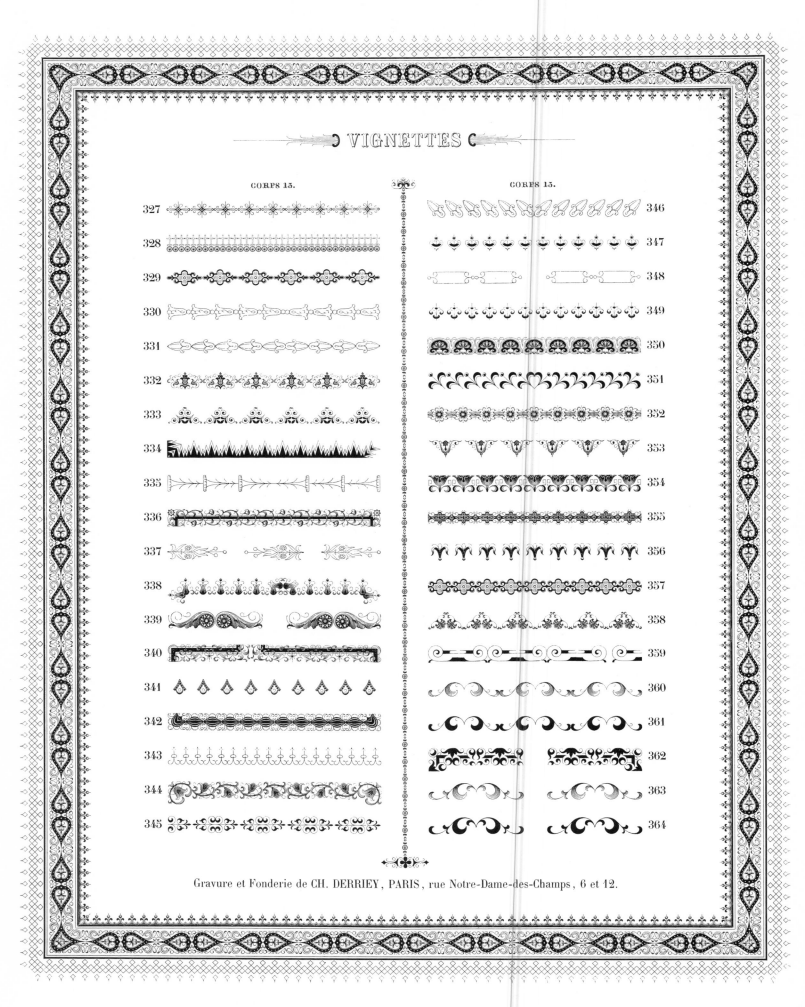

# VIGNETTES

CORPS 15.

CORPS 15.

327

328

329

330

331

332

333

334

335

336

337

338

339

340

341

342

343

344

345

346

347

348

349

350

351

352

353

354

355

356

357

358

359

360

361

362

363

364

Gravure et Fonderie de CH. DERRIEY, PARIS, rue Notre-Dame-des-Champs, 6 et 12.

**VIGNETTES**

CORPS 20.

CORPS 20.

365

381

366

382

367

383

368

384

369

385

370

386

371

387

372

388

373

389

374

390

375

391

376

392

377

393

378

394

379

395

380

396

*GRAVURE ET FONDERIE DE CH. DERRIEY, PARIS, RUE NOTRE-DAME-DES-CHAMPS, 6 ET 12.*

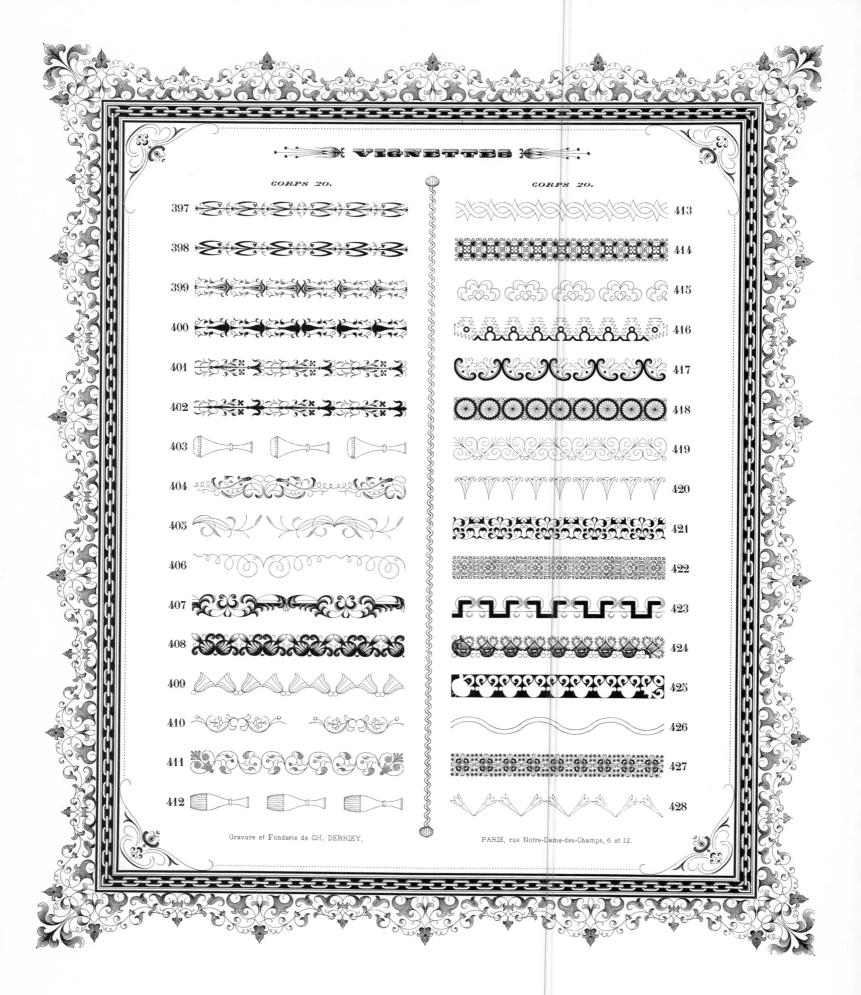

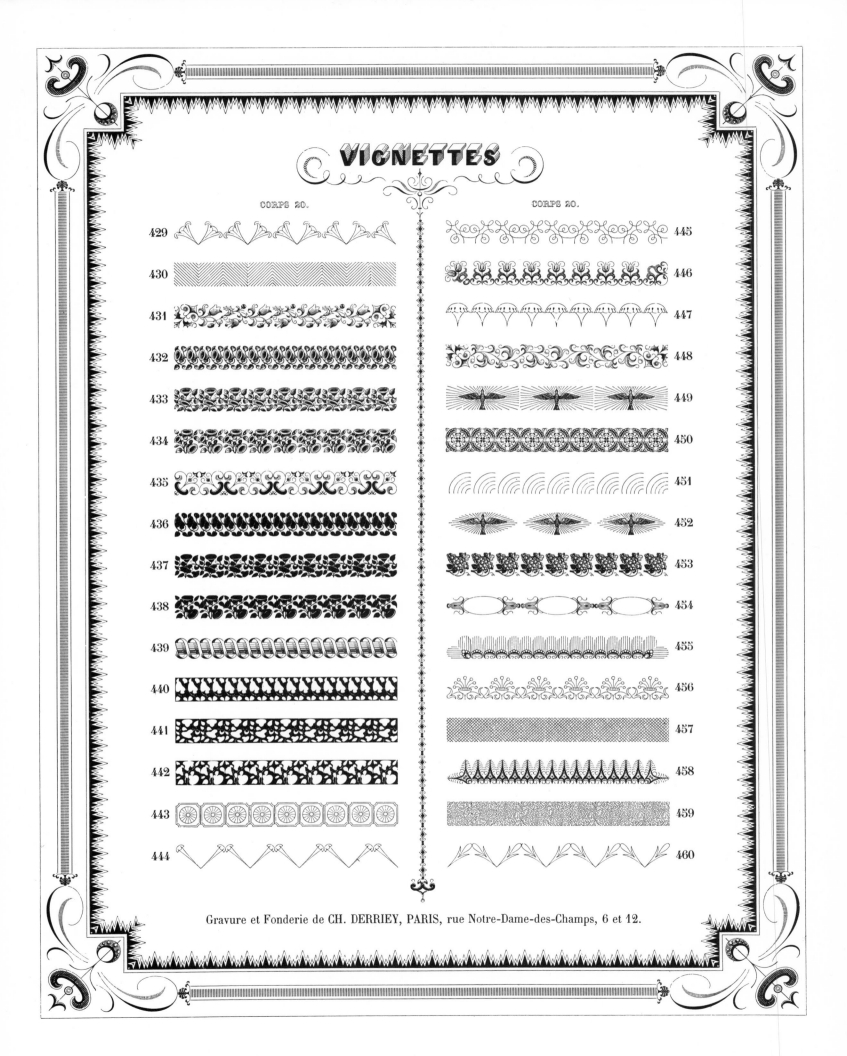

# VIGNETTES

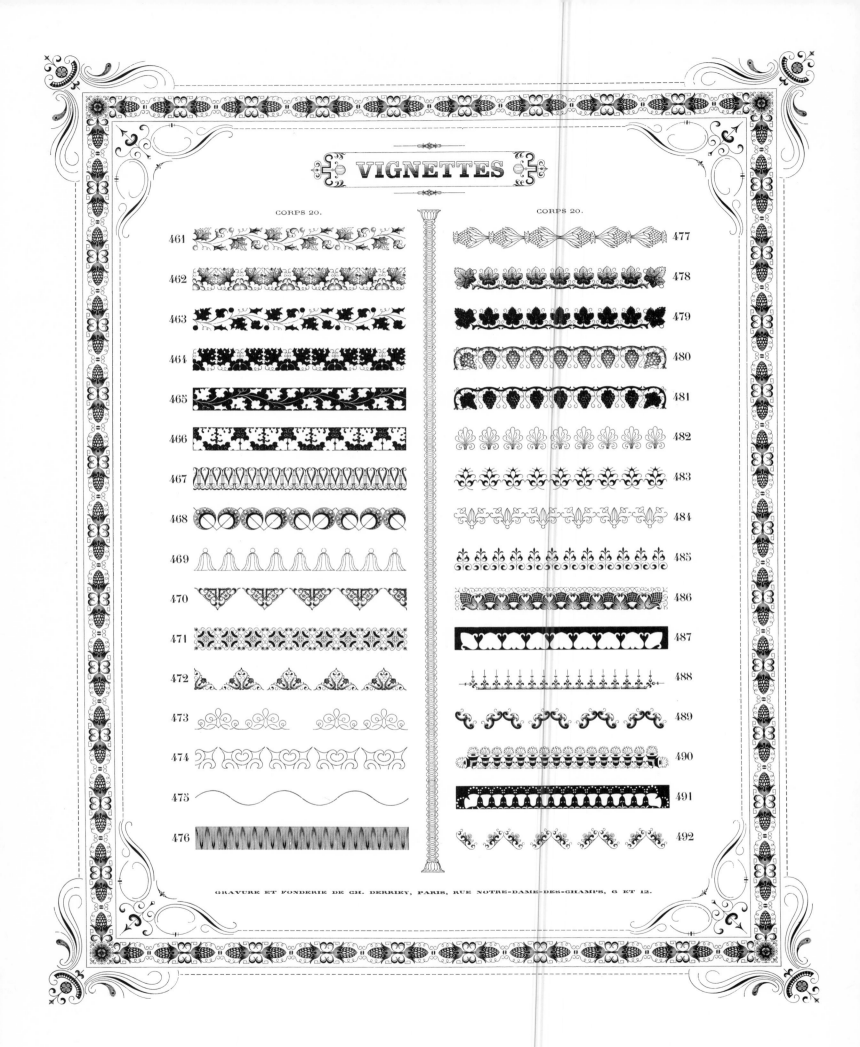

VIGNETTES

CORPS 20.

CORPS 20.

461 477
462 478
463 479
464 480
465 481
466 482
467 483
468 484
469 485
470 486
471 487
472 488
473 489
474 490
475 491
476 492

GRAVURE ET FONDERIE DE CH. DERRIEY, PARIS, RUE NOTRE-DAME-DES-CHAMPS, 6 ET 12.

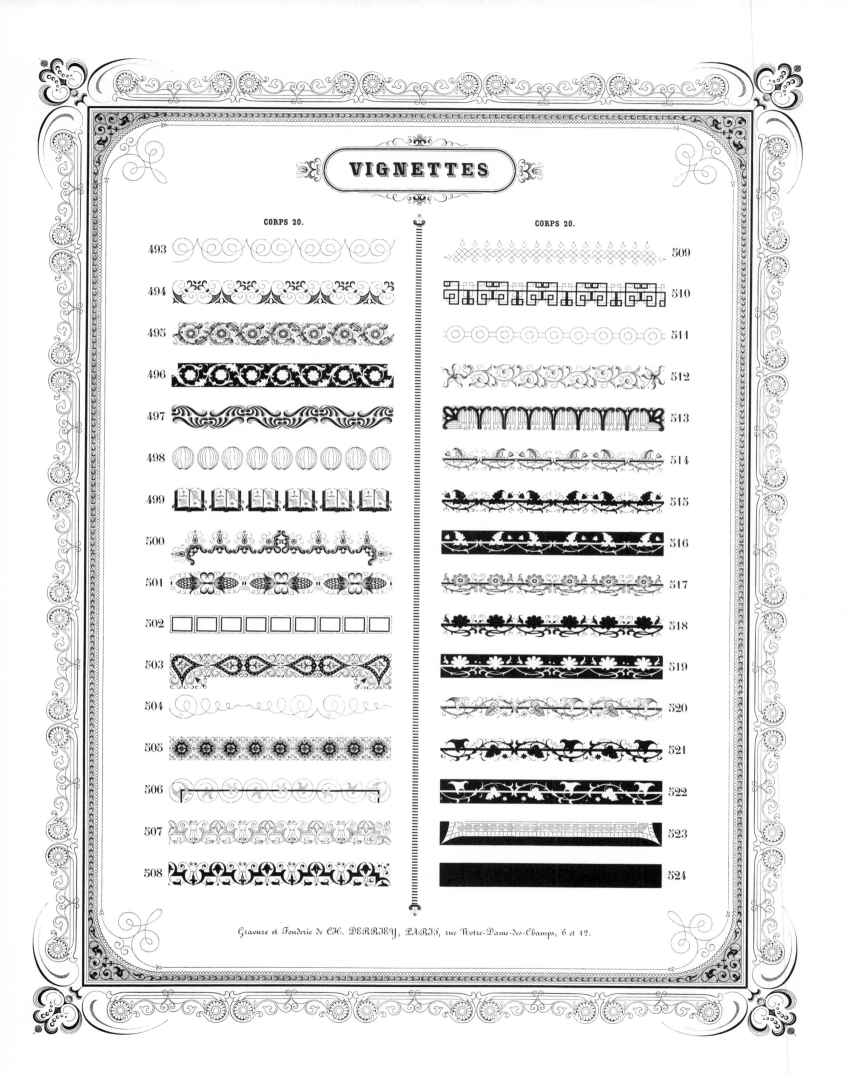

# VIGNETTES

CORPS 20.

CORPS 20.

Gravure et Fonderie de CH. DERRIEY, PARIS, rue Notre-Dame-des-Champs, 6 et 12.

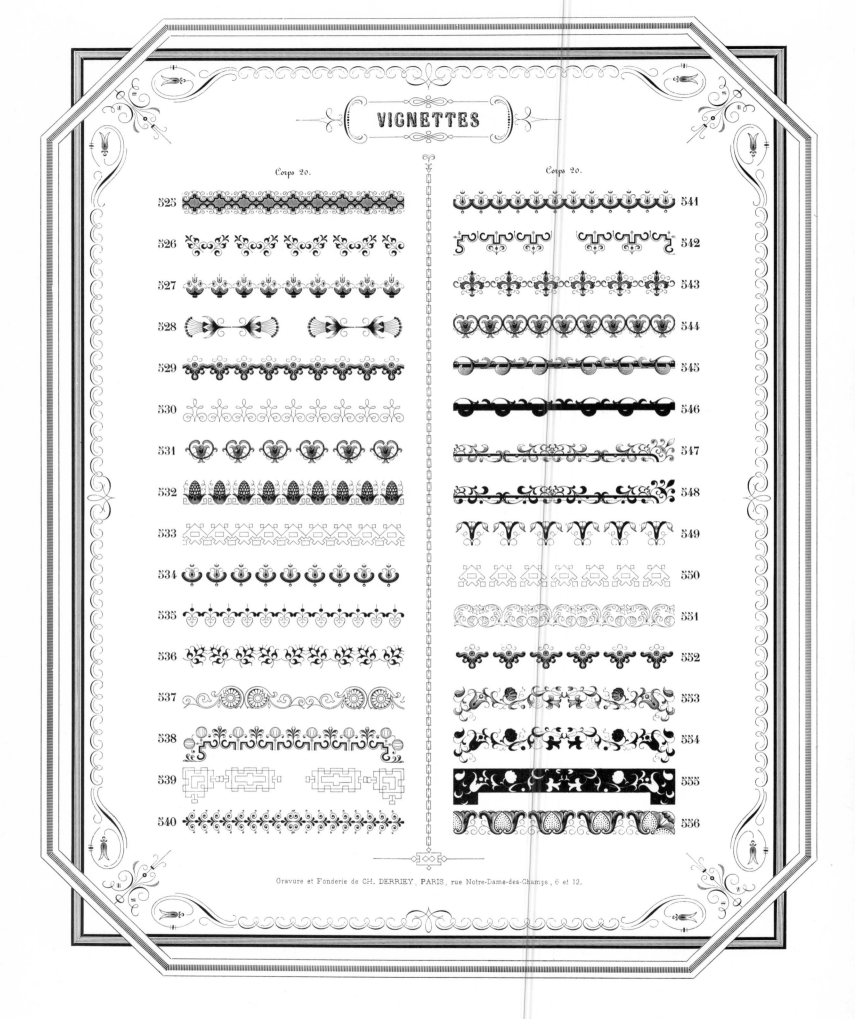

VIGNETTES

Corps 20.                                        Corps 20.

525                                              541
526                                              542
527                                              543
528                                              544
529                                              545
530                                              546
531                                              547
532                                              548
533                                              549
534                                              550
535                                              551
536                                              552
537                                              553
538                                              554
539                                              555
540                                              556

Gravure et Fonderie de CH. DERRIEY, PARIS, rue Notre-Dame-des-Champs, 6 et 12.

# VIGNETTES

**CORPS 20.**

557
558
559
560
561
562
563
564
565
566
567
568
569
570
571
572

**CORPS 25.**

573
574
575
576
577
578
579
580
581
582
583
584
585
586

Gravure et Fonderie de CH. DERRIEY, PARIS, rue Notre-Dame-des-Champs, 6 et 12.

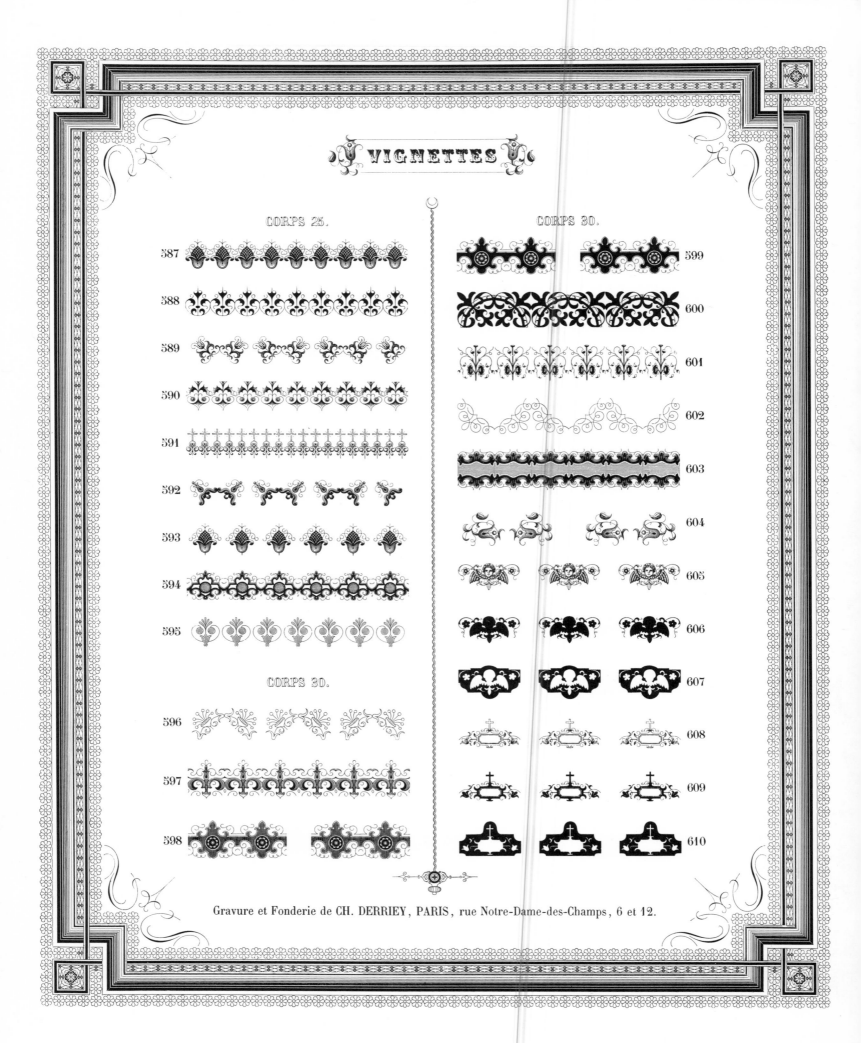

VIGNETTES

CORPS 25.

CORPS 30.

587

588

589

590

591

592

593

594

595

CORPS 30.

596

597

598

599

600

601

602

603

604

605

606

607

608

609

610

Gravure et Fonderie de CH. DERRIEY, PARIS, rue Notre-Dame-des-Champs, 6 et 12.

# VIGNETTES

CORPS 30

CORPS 30

611

612

613

614

615

616

617

618

619

620

621

622

623

624

625

626

627

628

629

630

631

632

633

634

635

636

Gravure et Fonderie de CH. DERRIEY,

PARIS, rue Notre-Dame-des-Champs, 6 et 12.

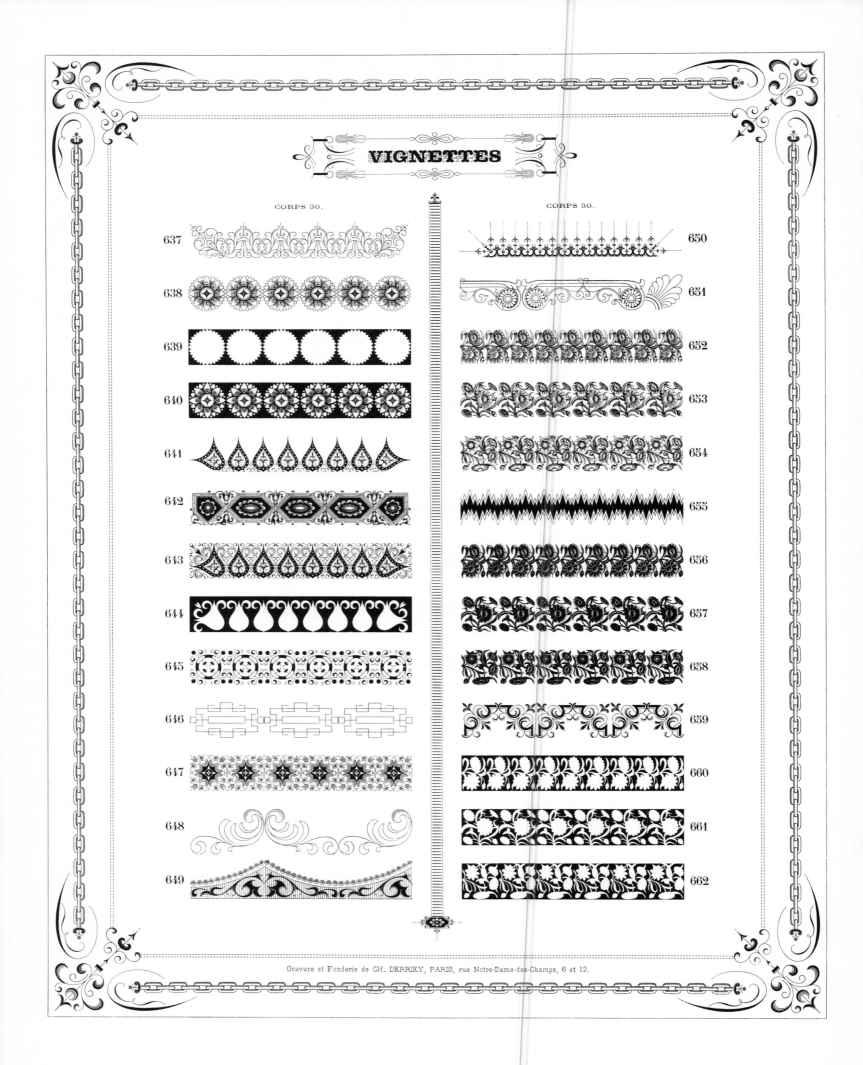

# VIGNETTES

CORPS 30.

CORPS 30.

637 638 639 640 641 642 643 644 645 646 647 648 649

650 651 652 653 654 655 656 657 658 659 660 661 662

Gravure et Fonderie de CH. DERRIEY, PARIS, rue Notre-Dame-des-Champs, 6 et 12.

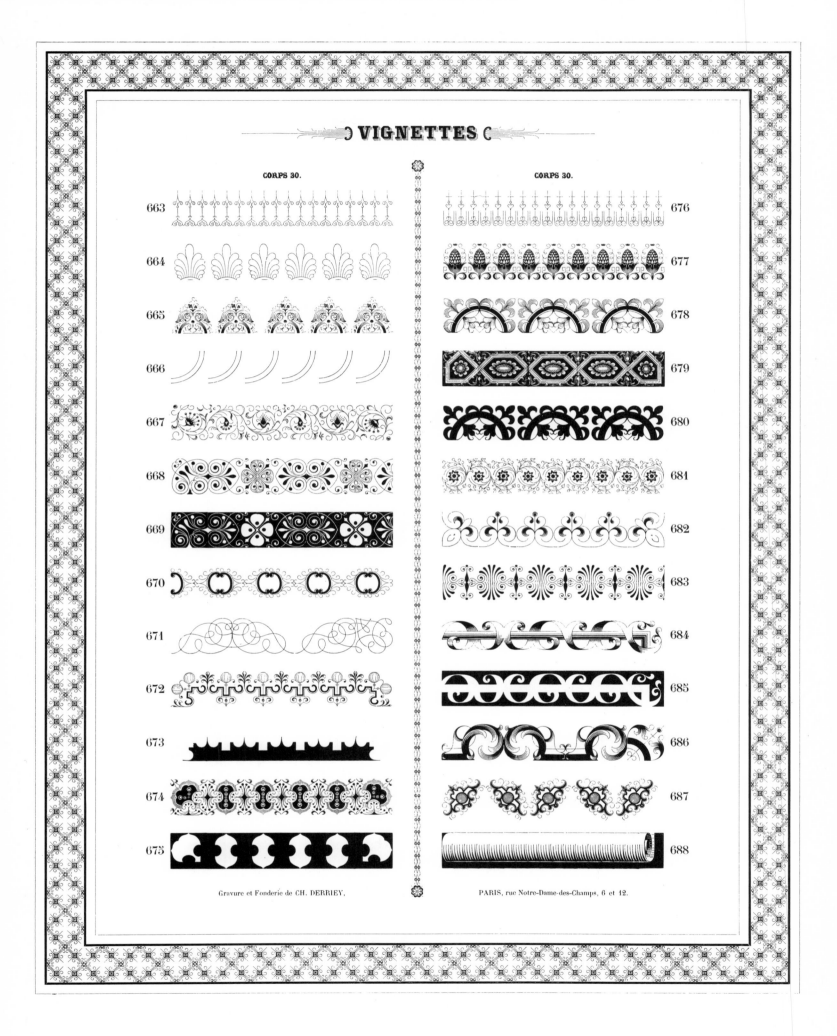

# VIGNETTES

CORPS 30.

663
664
665
666
667
668
669
670
671
672
673
674
675

CORPS 30.

676
677
678
679
680
681
682
683
684
685
686
687
688

Gravure et Fonderie de CH. DERRIEY.

PARIS, rue Notre-Dame-des-Champs, 6 et 12.

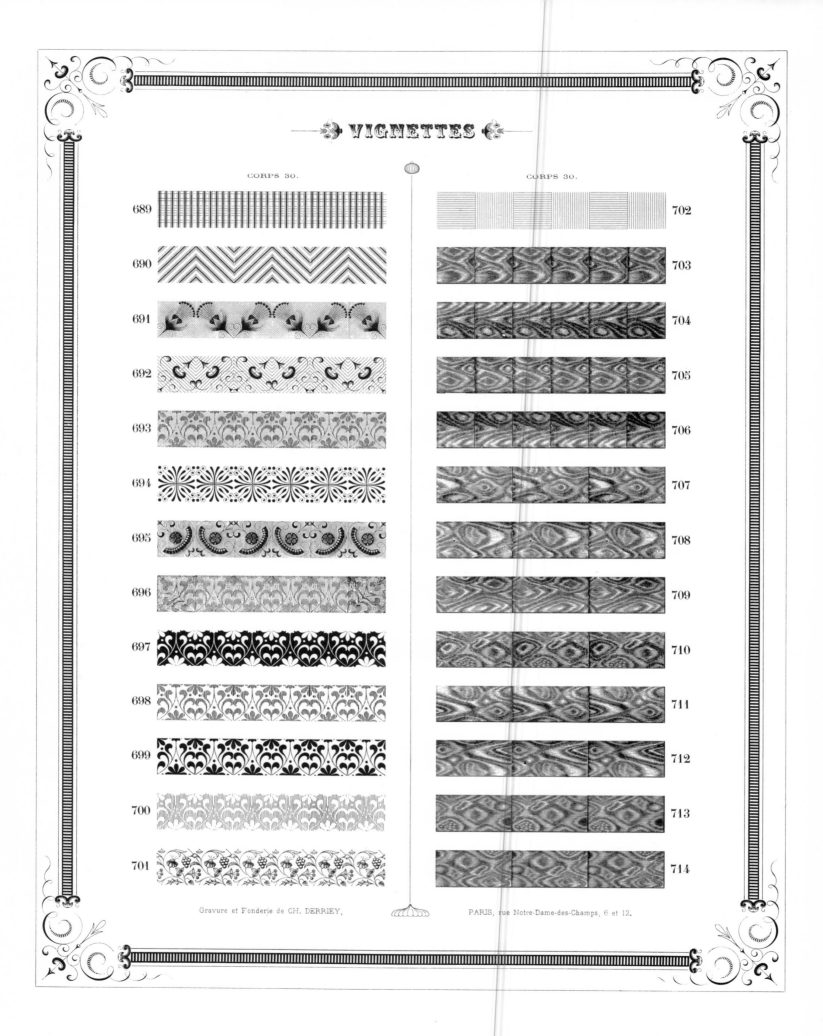

VIGNETTES

CORPS 30.

CORPS 30.

689 · 690 · 691 · 692 · 693 · 694 · 695 · 696 · 697 · 698 · 699 · 700 · 701

702 · 703 · 704 · 705 · 706 · 707 · 708 · 709 · 710 · 711 · 712 · 713 · 714

Gravure et Fonderie de CH. DERRIEY,    PARIS, rue Notre-Dame-des-Champs, 6 et 12.

20    Headpieces, Tailpieces and Border Elements

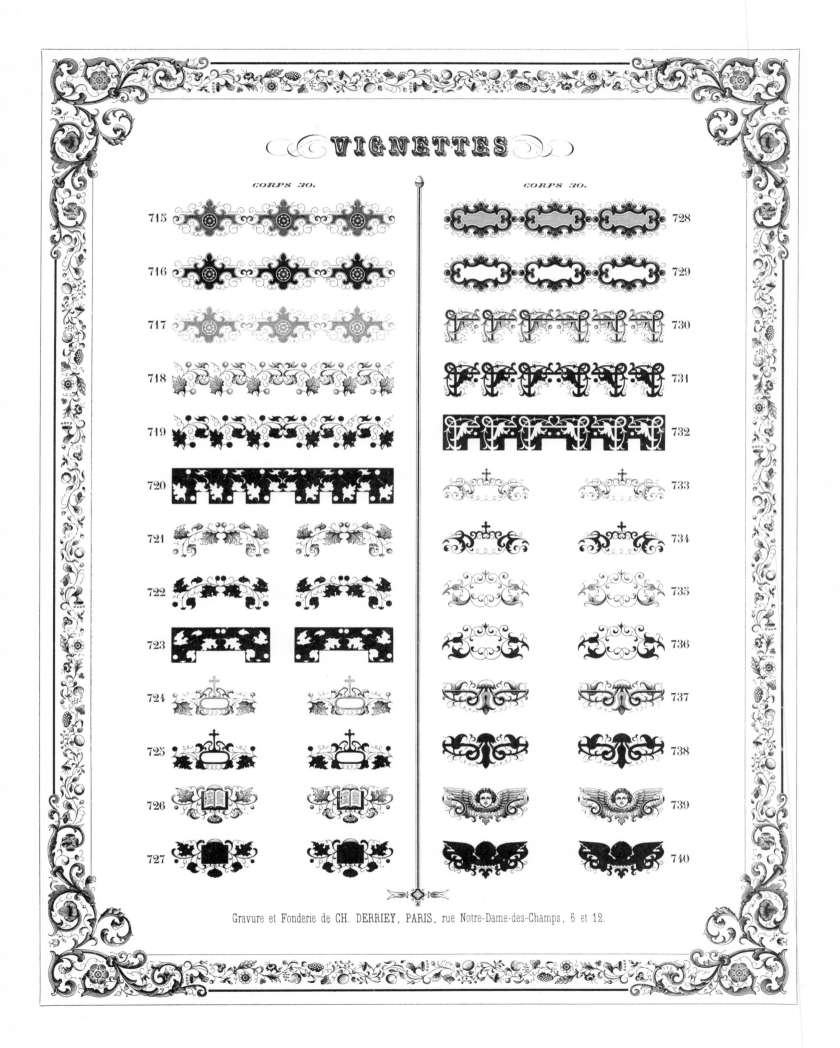

VIGNETTES

CORPS 30.

CORPS 30.

Gravure et Fonderie de CH. DERRIEY, PARIS, rue Notre-Dame-des-Champs, 6 et 12.

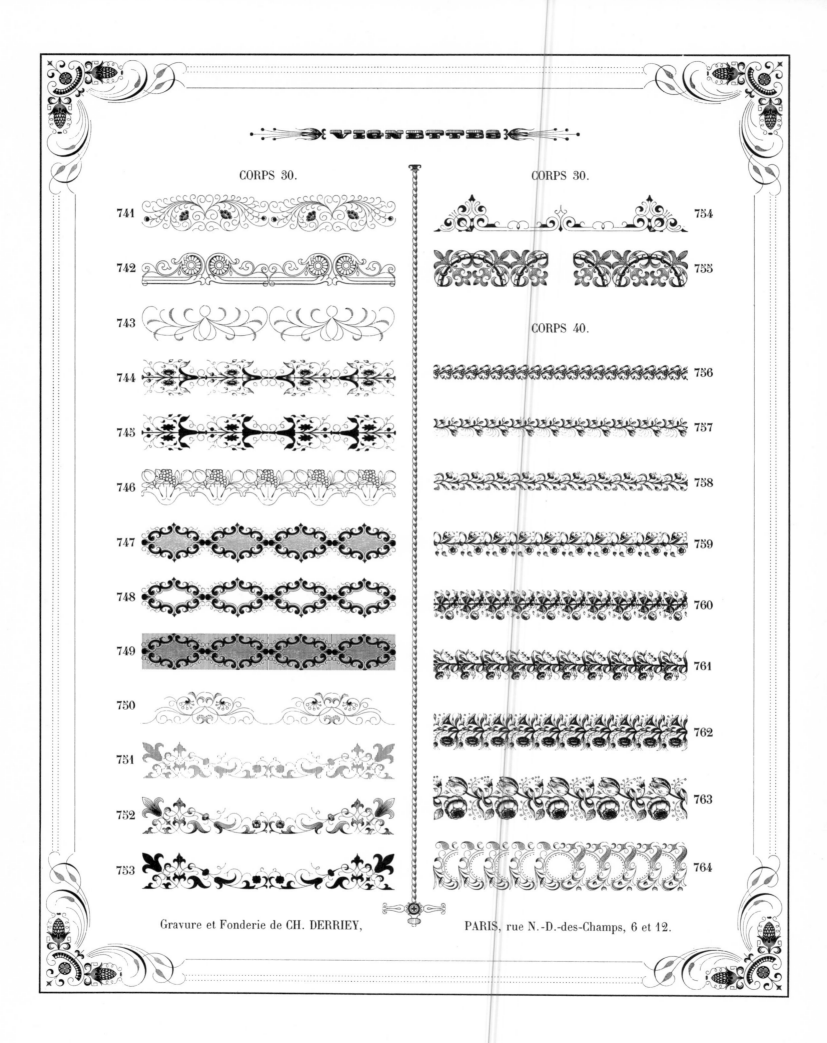

VIGNETTES

CORPS 30.

741
742
743
744
745
746
747
748
749
750
751
752
753

CORPS 30.

754
755

CORPS 40.

756
757
758
759
760
761
762
763
764

Gravure et Fonderie de CH. DERRIEY,          PARIS, rue N.-D.-des-Champs, 6 et 12.

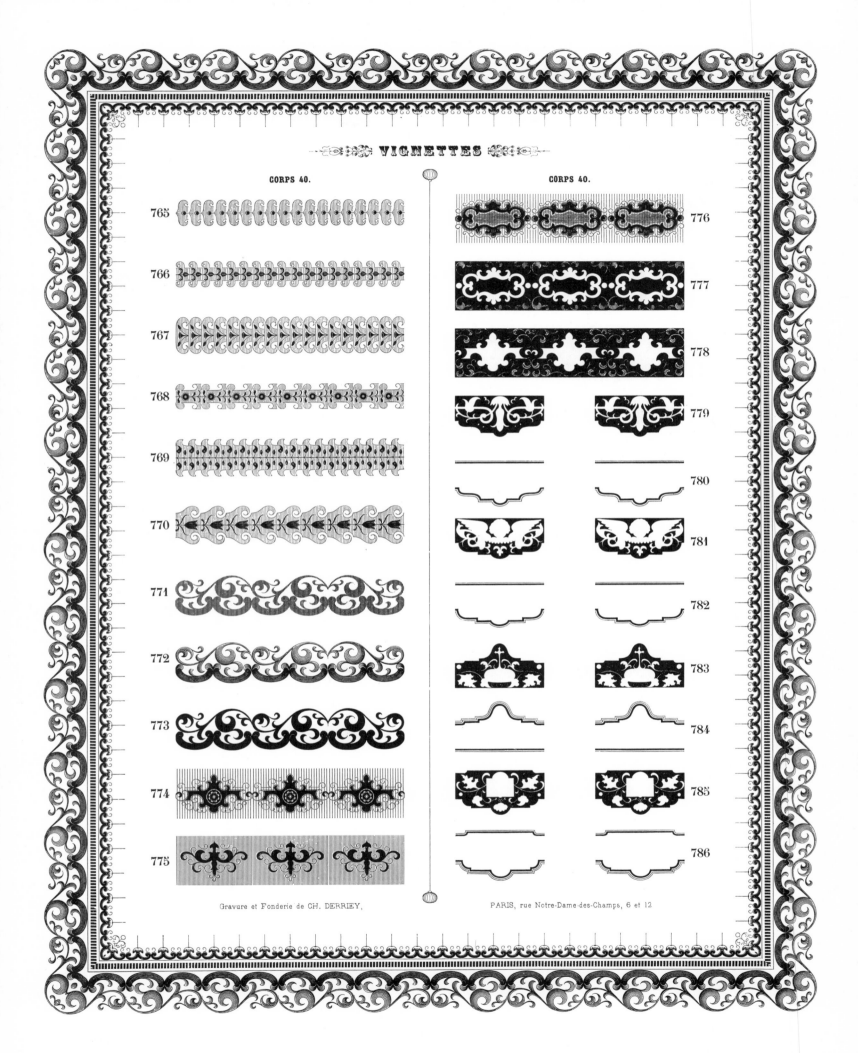

Corps 40.                    Corps 40.

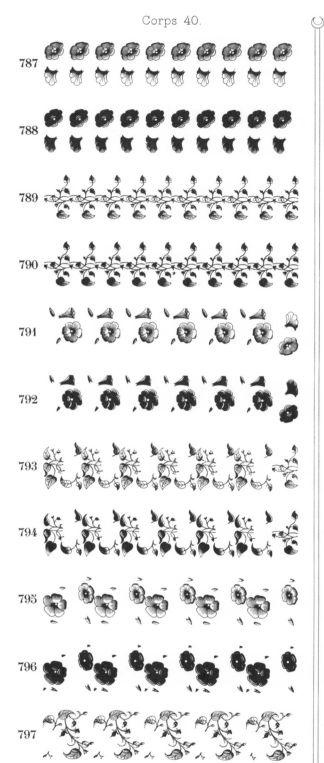

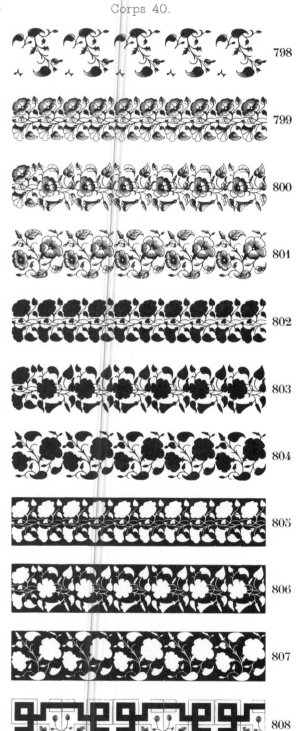

787

788

789

790

791

792

793

794

795

796

797

798

799

800

801

802

803

804

805

806

807

808

Gravure et Fonderie de CH. DERRIEY, PARIS, rue Notre-Dame-des-Champs, 6 et 12.

VIGNETTES

CORPS 40.    CORPS 40.

809    820
810    821
811    822
812    823
813    824
814    825
815    826
816    827
817    828
818    829
819    830

Gravure et Fonderie de CH. DERRIEY.    PARIS, rue Notre-Dame-des-Champs, 6 et 12.

# VIGNETTES

831

832

833

834

835

836

837

838

839

840

841

842

843

844

845

846

847

848

849

850

851

852

Gravure et Fonderie de CH. DERRIEY,  PARIS, rue Notre-Dame-des-Champs, 6 et 12.

VIGNETTES

CORPS 40.                    CORPS 40.

853
854
855
856
857
858
859
860
861
862
863

864
865
866
867
868
869
870
871
872
873
874

Gravure et Fonderie de CH. DERRIEY,          PARIS, rue Notre-Dame-des-Champs, 6 et 12.

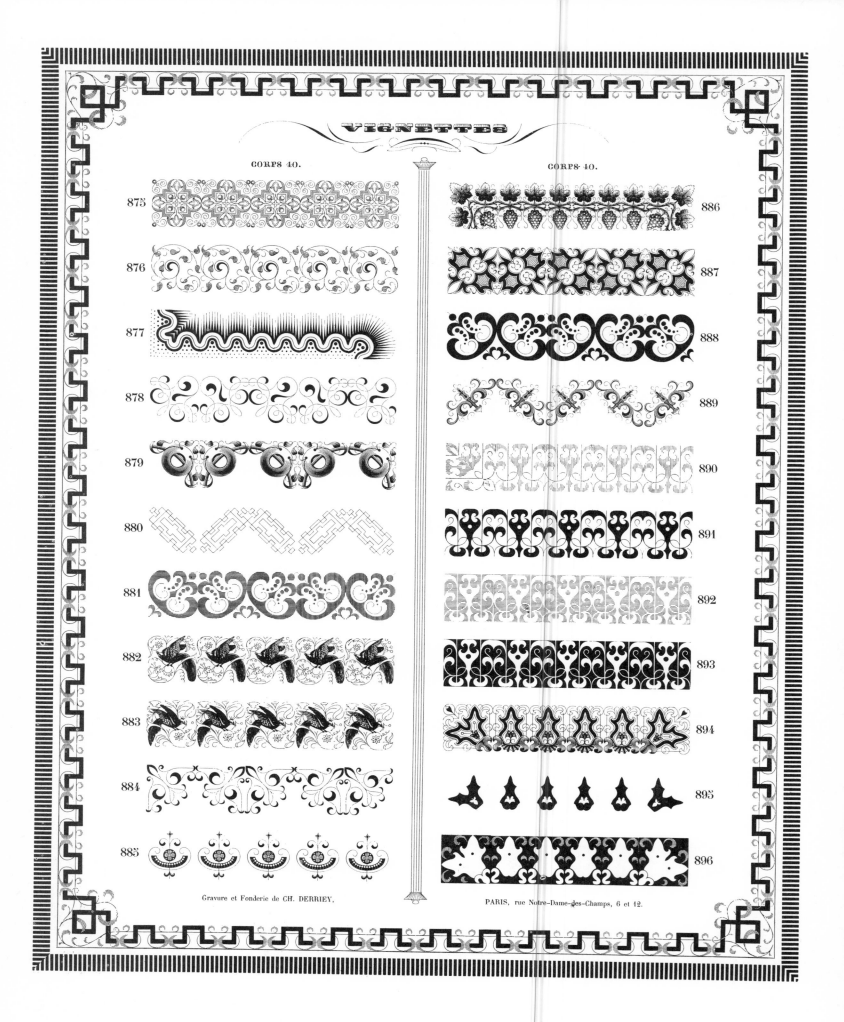

VIGNETTES

CORPS 40.

CORPS 40.

875

876

877

878

879

880

881

882

883

884

885

886

887

888

889

890

891

892

893

894

895

896

Gravure et Fonderie de CH. DERRIEY.

PARIS, rue Notre–Dame–des–Champs, 6 et 12.

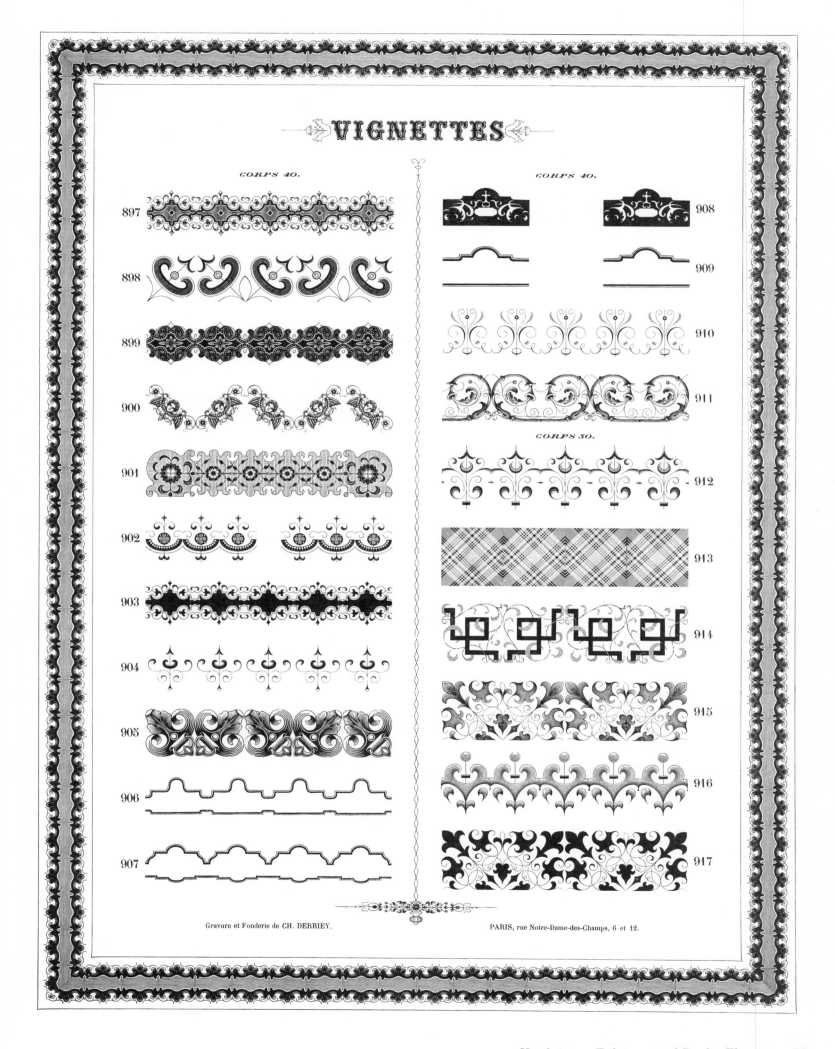

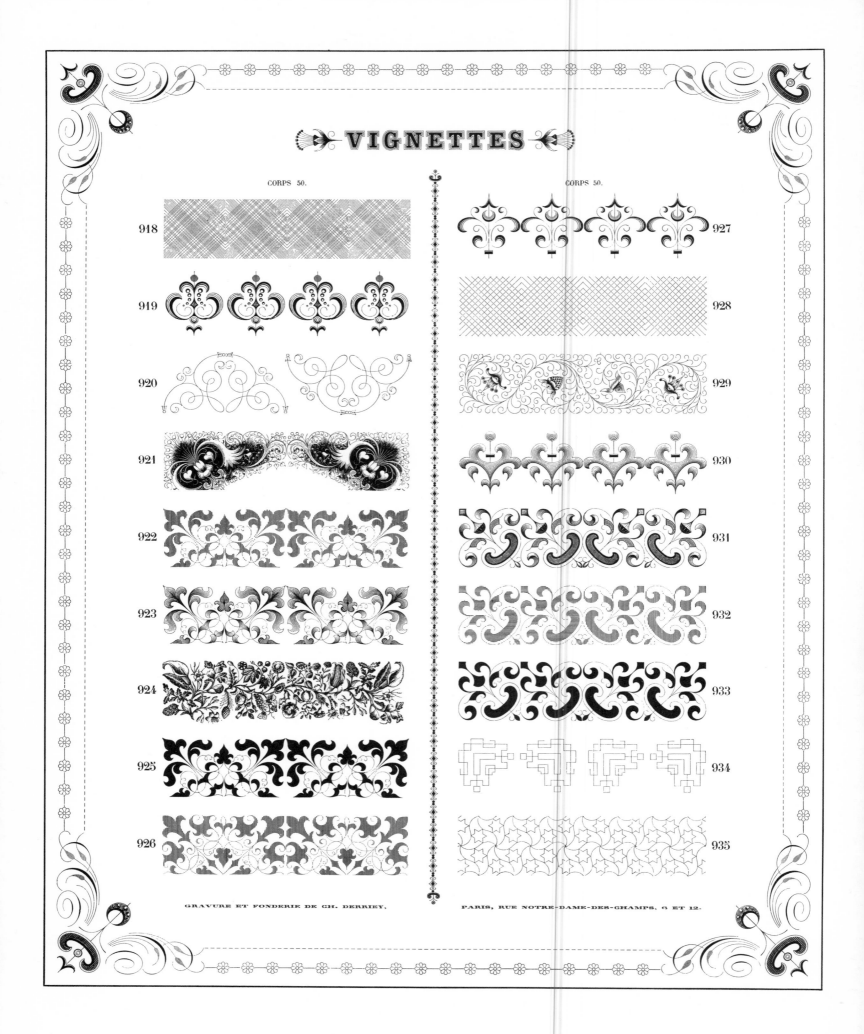

# VIGNETTES

CORPS 50.

CORPS 50.

918

919

920

921

922

923

924

925

926

927

928

929

930

931

932

933

934

935

GRAVURE ET FONDERIE DE CH. DERRIEY,    PARIS, RUE NOTRE-DAME-DES-CHAMPS, 6 ET 12.

VIGNETTES

CORPS 50.

936

937

938

939

CORPS 60.

940

941

942

943

CORPS 60.

944

945

946

947

948

949

950

951

Gravure et Fonderie de CH. DERRIEY,

PARIS, rue Notre-Dame-des-Champs, 6 et 12.

# VIGNETTES

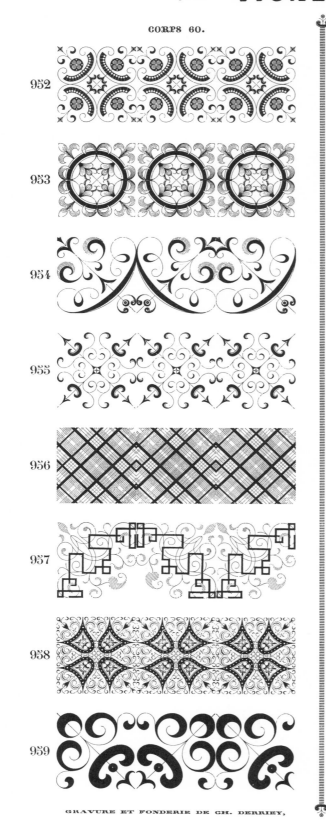

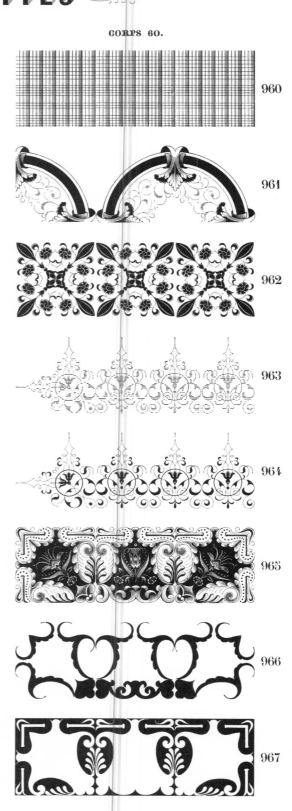

952
953
954
955
956
957
958
959

960
961
962
963
964
965
966
967

GRAVURE ET FONDERIE DE CH. DERRIEY,

PARIS, RUE N.-D.-DES-CHAMPS, 6 ET 12.

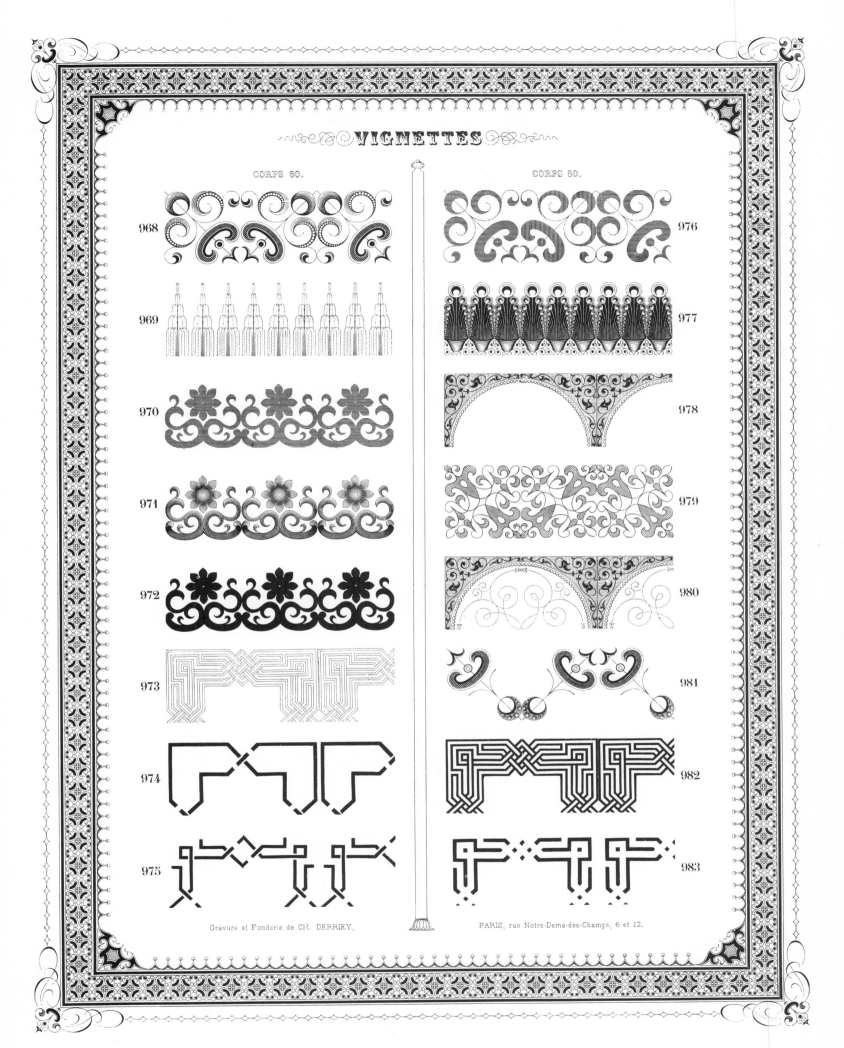

VIGNETTES

984

985

986

987

988

989

990          991

992

993

994

Gravure et Fonderie de CH. DERRIEY, PARIS, rue Notre-Dame-des-Champs, 6 et 12.

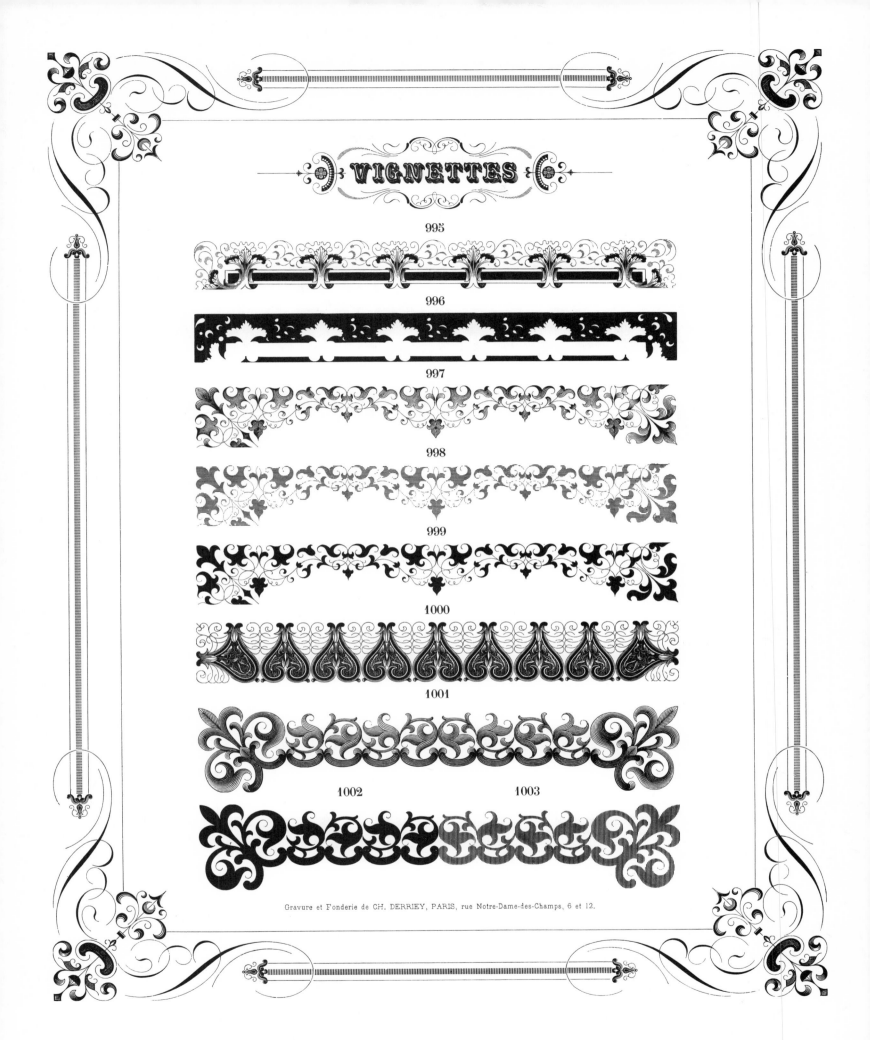

**VIGNETTES**

995

996

997

998

999

1000

1001

1002          1003

Gravure et Fonderie de CH. DERRIEY, PARIS, rue Notre-Dame-des-Champs, 6 et 12.

# VIGNETTES

1004

1005

1006

1007

1008

1009

1010

Gravure et Fonderie de CH. DERRIEY, PARIS, rue Notre-Dame-des-Champs, 6 et 12.

# VIGNETTES

1011

1012

1013        1014        1013

1015

1016

1017

1018

Gravure et Fonderie de CH. DERRIEY, PARIS, rue Notre-Dame-des-Champs, 6 et 12.

VIGNETTES

1019

1020

1021

1022

1023

1024

1025

Gravure et Fonderie de CH. DERRIEY, PARIS, rue Notre-Dame-des-Champs, 6 et 12.

# VIGNETTES

1026

1027

1028

1029

1030

1031

Gravure et Fonderie de CH. DERRIEY, PARIS, rue Notre-Dame-des-Champs, 6 et 12.

# VIGNETTES

**1032**

**1033**          **1034**

**1035**

**1036**

**1037**

Gravure et Fonderie de CH. DERRIEY, PARIS, rue Notre-Dame-des-Champs, 6 et 12.

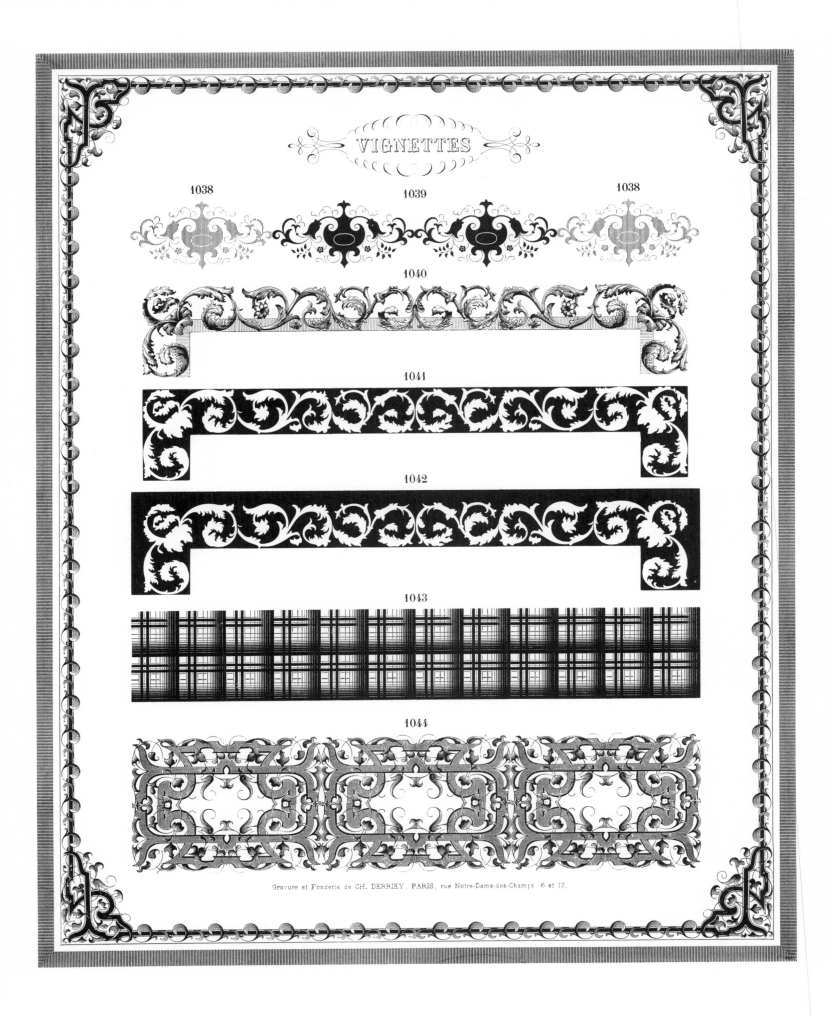

VIGNETTES

1038      1039      1038

1040

1041

1042

1043

1044

Gravure et Fonderie de CH. DERRIEY, PARIS, rue Notre-Dame-des-Champs 6 et 12.

**VIGNETTES**

1045

1046     1047     1046

1048     1049     1048

1050

1051

1052

Gravure et Fonderie de CH. DERRIEY, PARIS, rue Notre-Dame-des-Champs, 6 et 12.

# VIGNETTES

### 1053

### 1054

### 1055

### 1056

### 1057

### 1058

Gravure et Fonderie de CH. DERRIEY, PARIS, rue Notre-Dame-des-Champs, 6 et 12.

**VIGNETTES**

1059

1060

1061

1062

1063

Gravure et Fonderie de CH. DERRIEY, PARIS, rue Notre-Dame-des-Champs, 6 et 12.

# CARACTÈRES ORNÉS

Nº 1.

EXERÇANT AVEC PROBITÉ SON TALENT OU SON INDUSTRIE

Nº 2.

AIDÉ DE L'ÉTUDE, DU TRAVAIL ET DE LA PERSÉVÉRANCE

Nº 3.

IL NE FAUT PAS TOUJOURS DIRE CE QU'ON PENSE

Nº 4.

HASARDEZ UN PREMIER EFFORT, RENOUVELEZ LA TENTATIVE

Nº 5.

LA BIENFAISANCE EST UNE VERTU QUI TROUVE

Nº 6.

UN COURTISAN, HOMME SANS MÉRITE

Nº 7.

## COUPOIR A BISEAUTER

Nº 8.

# COMPAGNIE

Nº 9.

# LA PROVIDENCE

Gravure et Fonderie de CH. DERRIEY, PARIS, rue Notre-Dame-des-Champs, 6 et 12.

**CARACTÈRES ORNÉS**

Nº 10.

AU BUT QUI SEMBLE FUIR D'ABORD

Nº 11.

A NOS YEUX UN NUAGE SOMBRE CACHE LES RAYONS DU BONHEUR

Nº 12.

LE LION AMOUREUX

Nº 13.

## NAPOLÉON III EMPEREUR

Nº 14.

HONORONS CE NOBLE CIVISME

Nº 15.

IMPRESSION DE MUSIQUE

Nº 16.

RIEN N'EST SI RARE QUE LA CHOSE

Nº 17.

## L'ARMÉE D'ITALIE

Nº 18.

TRAITS DE PLUME

Gravure et Fonderie de CH. DERRIEY, PARIS, rue N.-D.-des-Champs, 6 et 12.

### · CARACTÈRES ORNÉS ·

N° 19

N'AI-JE PAS, SANS Y PENSER, LAISSÉ ÉCHAPPER QUELQUE SOTTISE ?

N° 20.

TU PRISES UN VIL MÉTAL SORTI DE LA TERRE

N° 21.

ALORS DANS VOS RÊVES DE GLOIRE

N° 22.

GLORIEUSE FRANCE

N° 23.

LA FONDERIE TYPOGRAPHIQUE

N° 24.

NAPOLÉON

N° 25.

IMPRIMERIE IMPÉRIALE DE

N° 26.

PHOTOGRAPHIE

Gravure et Fonderie de CH. DERRIEY, PARIS, rue Notre-Dame-des-Champs, 6 et 12.

CARACTÈRES ORNÉS

N° 27.

SAISISSEZ D'UNE MAIN FERME LES JALONS QUI

N° 28.

SOCIÉTÉ INTERNATIONALE

N° 29.

LE COMMENCEMENT DU MONDE

N° 30.

LA GALVANOPLASTIE EST

N° 31.

CHEMINS DE FER ROMAINS

N° 32.

GUTENBERG

N° 33.

MANDEMENT

Gravure et Fonderie de CH. DERRIEY, PARIS, rue Notre-Dame-des-Champs, 6 et 12.

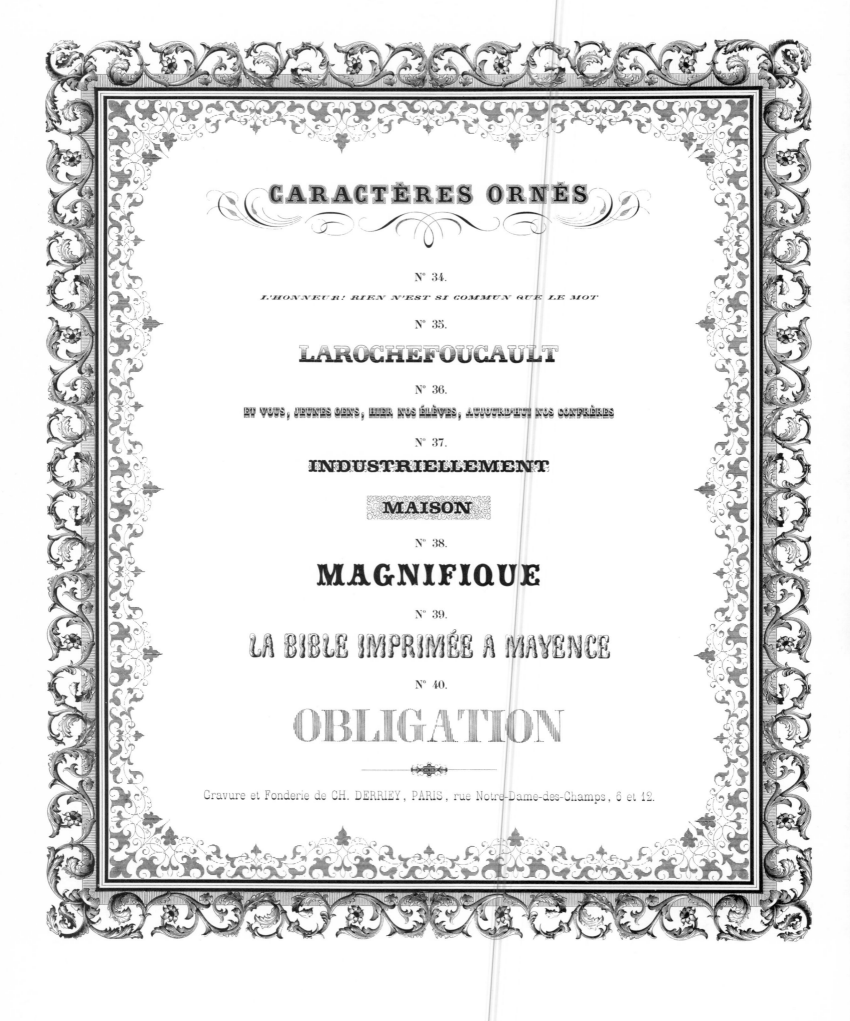

CARACTÈRES ORNÉS

N° 34.

L'HONNEUR! RIEN N'EST SI COMMUN QUE LE MOT

N° 35.

LAROCHEFOUCAULT

N° 36.

ET VOUS, JEUNES GENS, HIER NOS ÉLÈVES, AUJOURD'HUI NOS CONFRÈRES

N° 37.

INDUSTRIELLEMENT

MAISON

N° 38.

MAGNIFIQUE

N° 39.

LA BIBLE IMPRIMÉE A MAYENCE

N° 40.

OBLIGATION

Gravure et Fonderie de CH. DERRIEY, PARIS, rue Notre-Dame-des-Champs, 6 et 12.

**CARACTÈRES ORNÉS**

Nº 41.

**RÉGLURE S'IMPRIMANT AVEC LE TEXTE, PAR DERRIEY**

Nº 42.

**COMPTOIR NATIONAL**

Nº 43.

*LE SOMNIBUS DE LONDRES*

Nº 44.

**CONSTANTINOPLE**

Nº 45.

**LE TEMPS EST TROP LONG POUR LE PLAISIR**

Nº 46.

**CORDIALEMENT**

Nº 47.

**INTERNATIONAL**

Nº 48.

**ENCOURAGEMENT**

Gravure et Fonderie de C. DERRIEY, PARIS, rue Notre-Dame-des-Champs, 6 et 12.

CARACTÈRES ORNÉS

N° 49.

COMPAGNIE D'ASSURA

N° 50.

LES HARMONIES

N° 51.

COLONISATION

N° 52.

EUGÉNIE

N° 53.

CHEMIN DE FER DU NORD

Gravure et Fonderie de C. DERRIEY, PARIS, rue Notre-Dame-des-Champs, 6 et 12.

CARACTÈRES ORNÉS

N° 54.

LES CHARBONS DE MONS

N° 55.

BRIANÇON

N° 56.

FIRMIN DIDOT

N° 57.

RENTRURE

N° 58.

LE TYPOGRAPHE

Gravure et Fonderie de CH. DERRIEY, PARIS, rue Notre-Dame-des-Champs, 6 et 12.

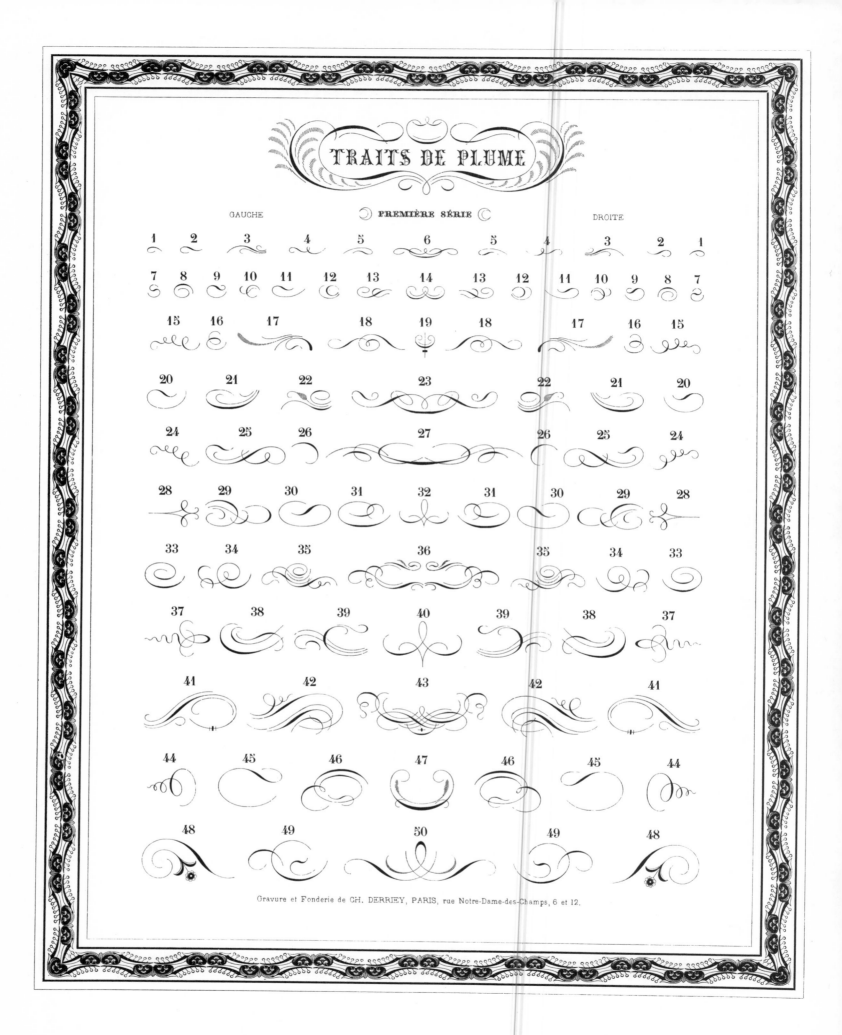

# TRAITS DE PLUME

GAUCHE DROITE

72 73 74 73 72

75 76 75

77

78

79 80 79

81 82 81

Gravure et Fonderie de CH. DERRIEY, PARIS, rue Notre-Dame-des-Champs, 6 et 12.

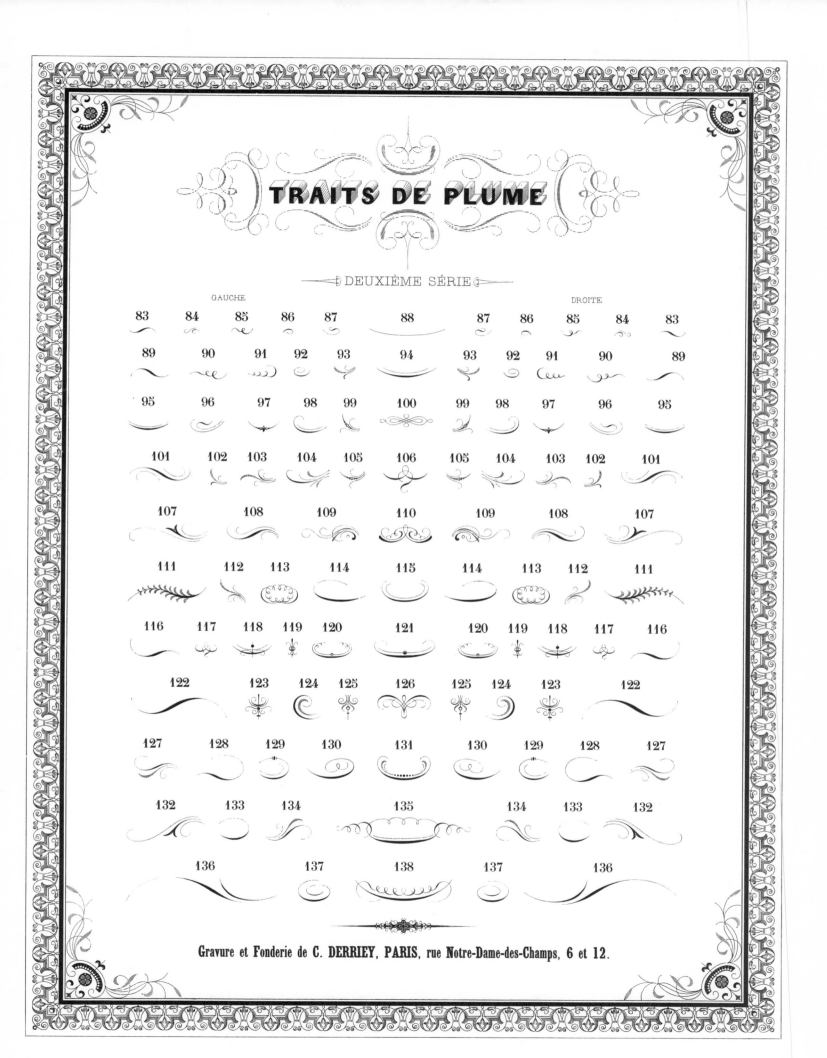

# TRAITS DE PLUME

DEUXIÈME SÉRIE

GAUCHE

DROITE

Gravure et Fonderie de C. DERRIEY, PARIS, rue Notre-Dame-des-Champs, 6 et 12.

TRAITS DE PLUME

TRAITS DE PLUME

**TRAITS DE PLUME**

GAUCHE                                DROITE

186

185                                        185

188

187                                       187

190

189                                       189

191                                     191

192

193                          194                   193

195

196

Gravure et Fonderie de CH. DERRIEY, PARIS, rue Notre-Dame-des-Champs, 6 et 12.

GAUCHE                                                  DROITE

Gravure et Fonderie de CH. DERRIEY, PARIS, rue Notre-Dame-des-Champs, 6 et 12.

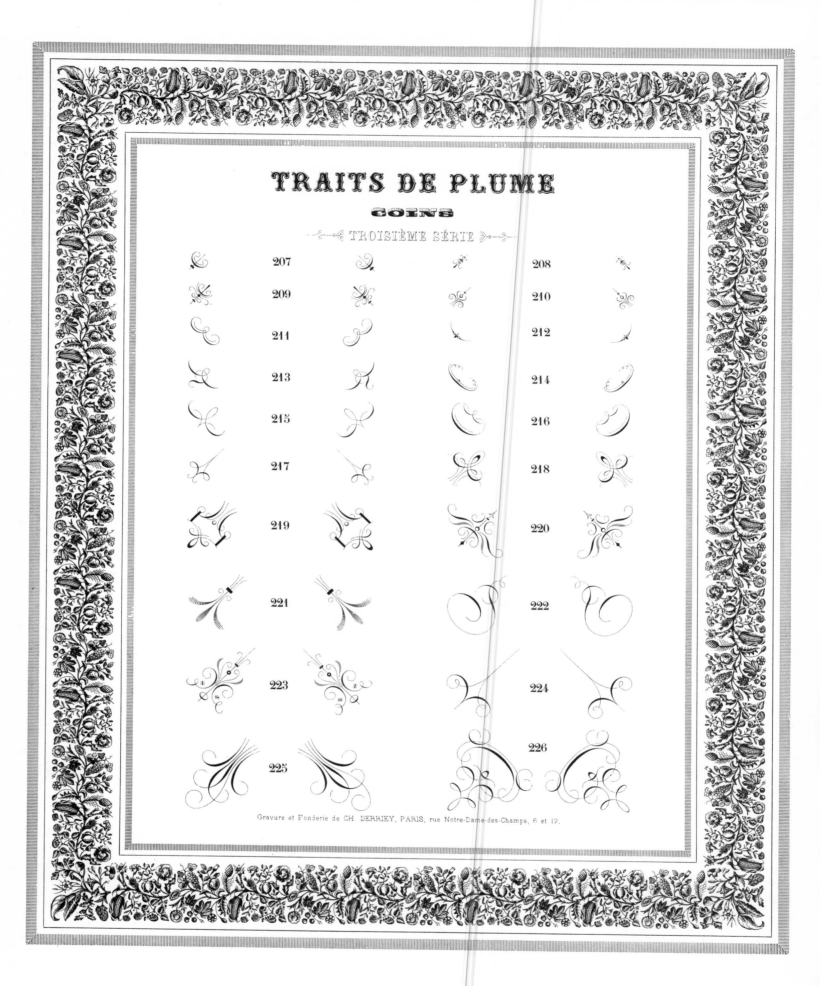

# TRAITS DE PLUME

## COINS

### TROISIÈME SÉRIE

207     208

209     210

211     212

213     214

215     216

217     218

219     220

221     222

223     224

226

225

Gravure et Fonderie de CH. DERRIEY, PARIS, rue Notre-Dame-des-Champs, 6 et 12.

# TRAITS DE PLUME

## COINS

227    228
229    230
231    232
233    234
235    236
237    238
239    240
241    242
243    244

Gravure et Fonderie de CH. DERRIEY, PARIS, rue Notre-Dame-des-Champs, 6 et 12.

GRAVURE ET FONDERIE

DE

C. DERRIEY

COINS COMPOSÉS

Rue Notre-Dame-des-Champs, 6 et 12.

PARIS

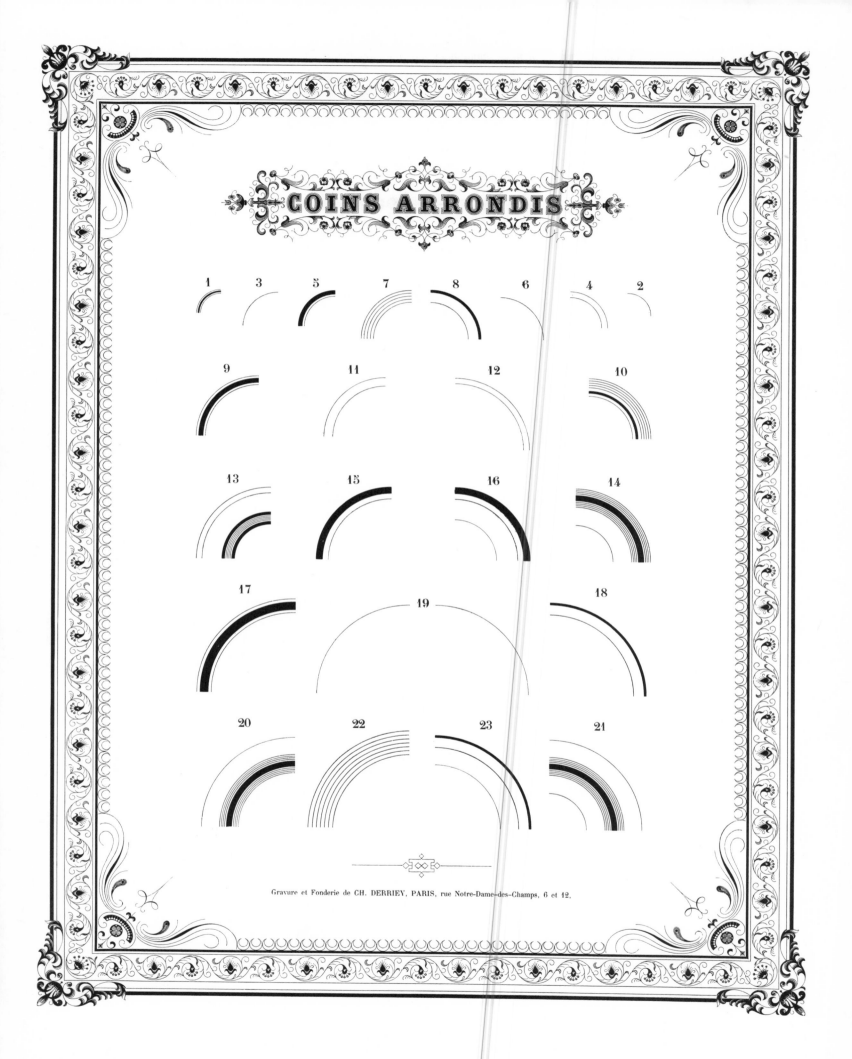

COINS ARRONDIS

Gravure et Fonderie de CH. DERRIEY, PARIS, rue Notre-Dame-des-Champs, 6 et 12.

# COINS

Gravure et Fonderie de CH. DERRIEY, PARIS, rue Notre-Dame-des-Champs, 6 et 12.

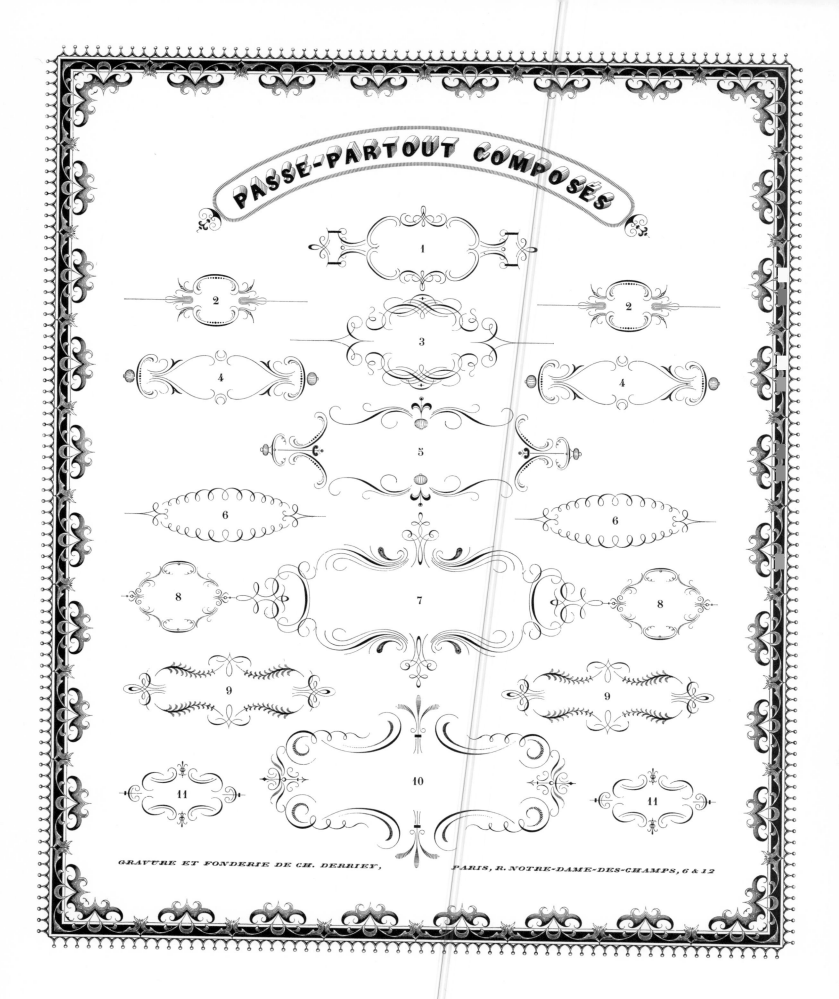

PASSE-PARTOUT COMPOSÉS

GRAVURE ET FONDERIE DE CH. DERRIEY, PARIS, R. NOTRE-DAME-DES-CHAMPS, 6 & 12

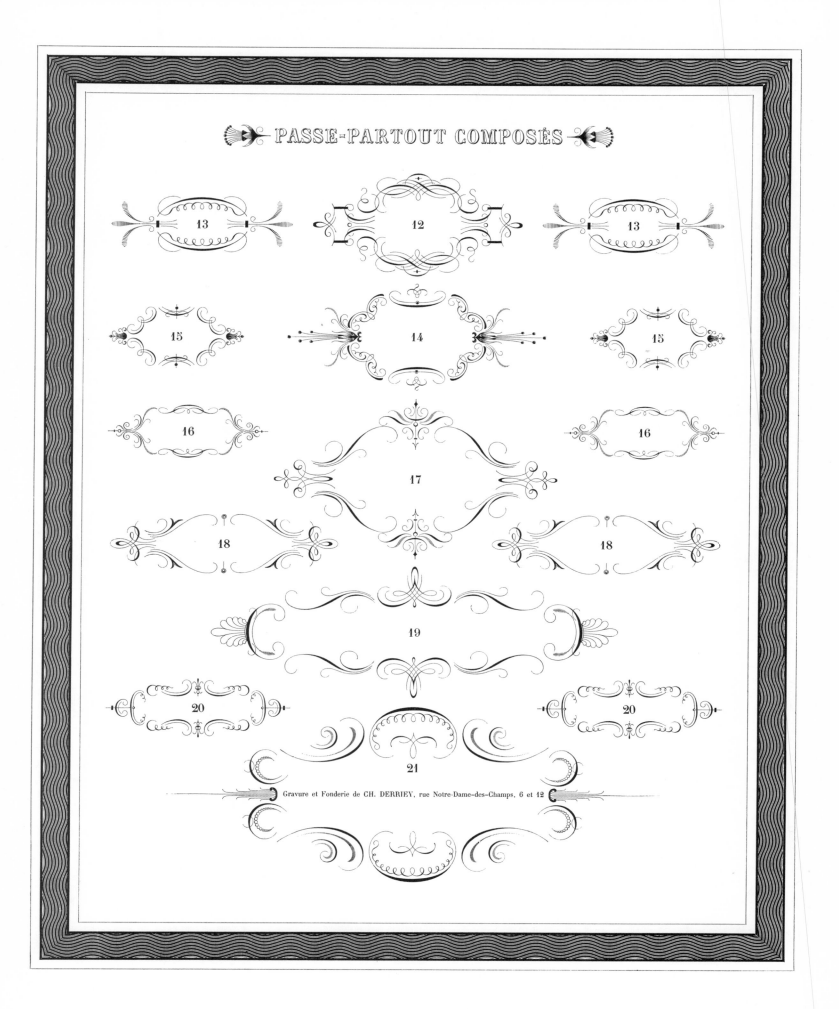

Gravure et Fonderie de CH. DERRIEY, PARIS, rue Notre-Dame-des-Champs, 6 et 12.

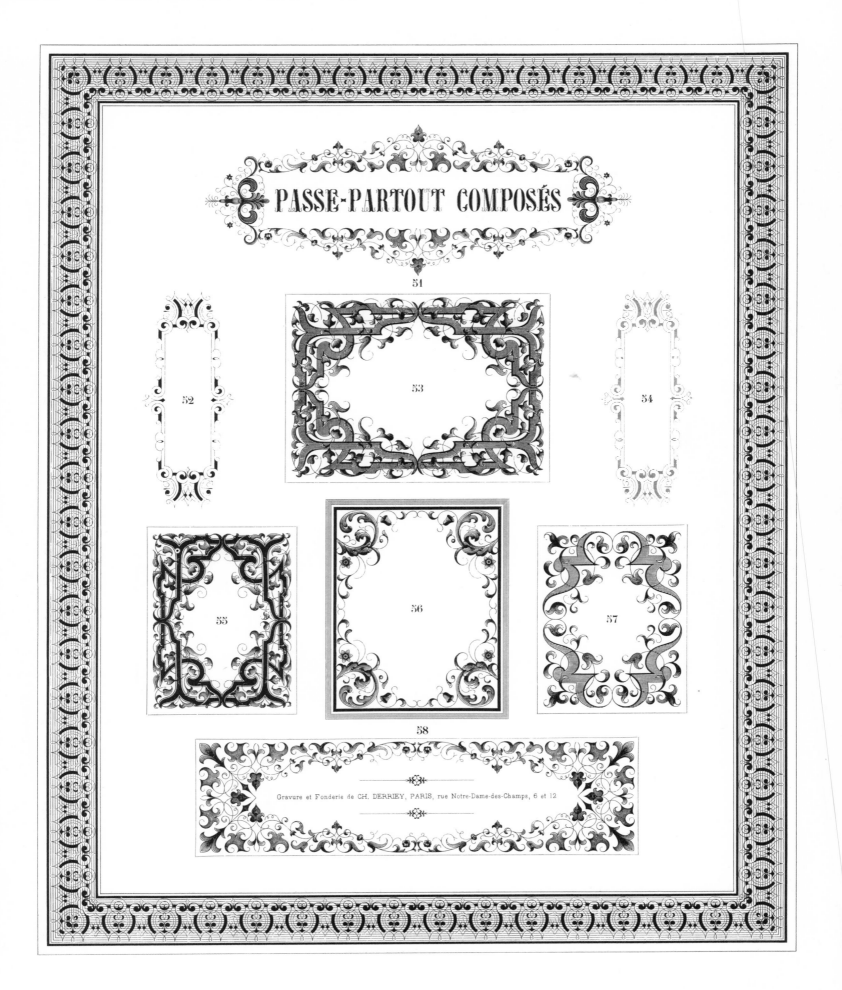

PASSE-PARTOUT COMPOSÉS

Gravure et Fonderie de CH. DERRIEY, PARIS, rue Notre-Dame-des-Champs, 6 et 12

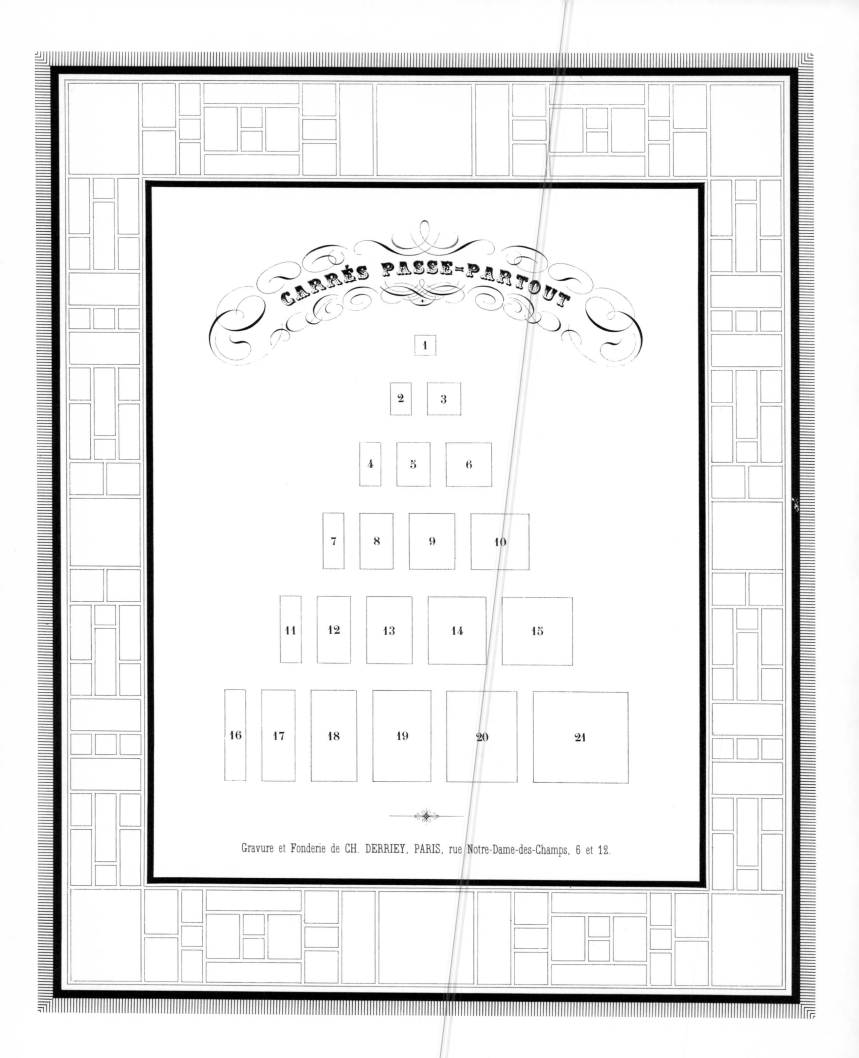

CARRÉS PASSE-PARTOUT

Gravure et Fonderie de CH. DERRIEY, PARIS, rue Notre-Dame-des-Champs, 6 et 12.

# RONDS PASSE-PARTOUT

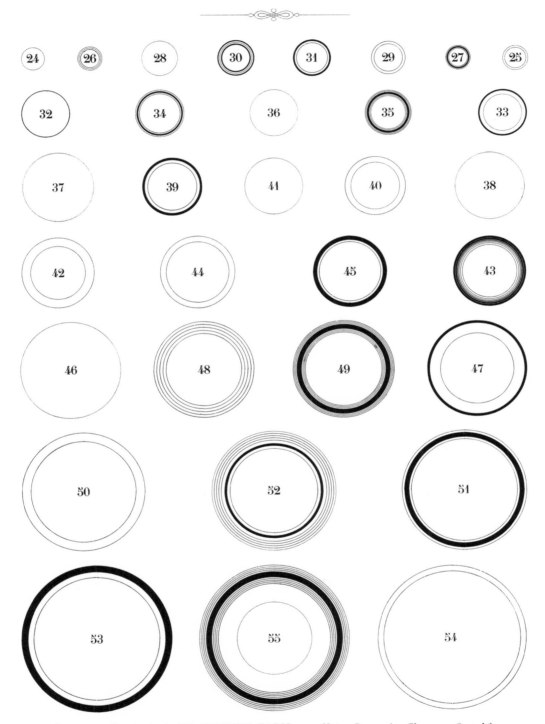

Gravure et Fonderie de CH. DERRIEY, PARIS, rue Notre-Dame-des-Champs, 6 et 12.

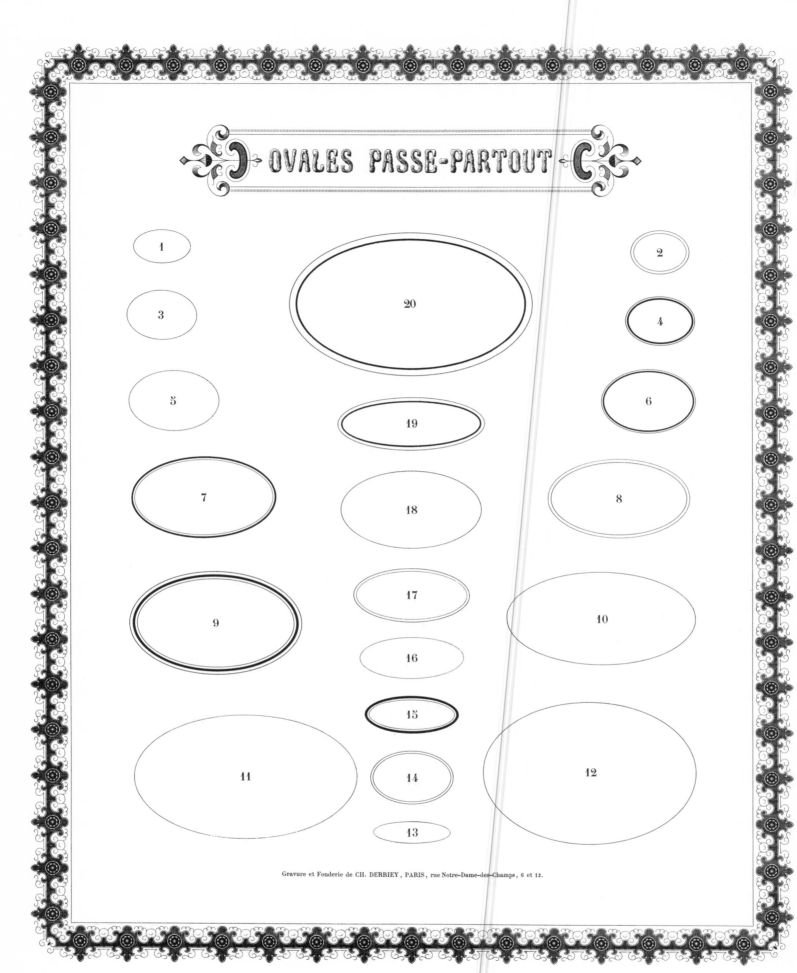

OVALES PASSE-PARTOUT

Gravure et Fonderie de CH. DERRIEY, PARIS, rue Notre-Dame-des-Champs, 6 et 12.

# PASSE-PARTOUT RONDS ET OVALES

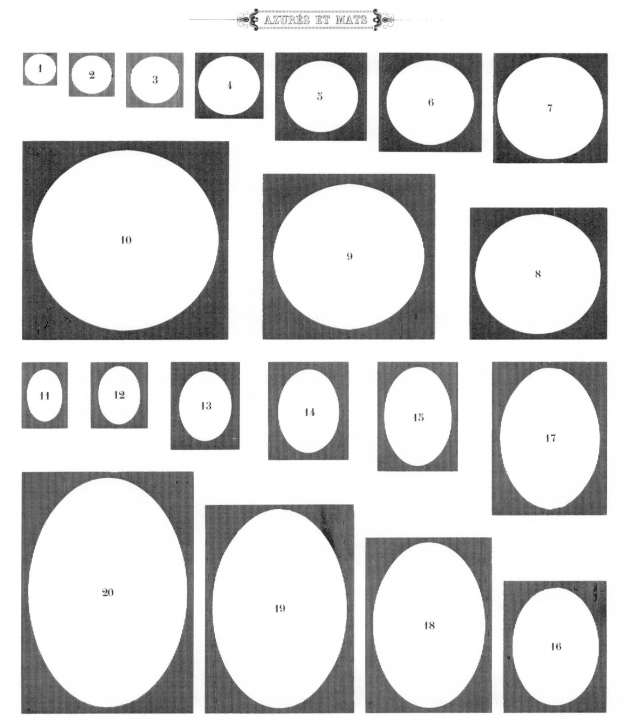

GRAVURE ET FONDERIE DE CH. DERRIEY, PARIS, RUE NOTRE-DAME-DES-CHAMPS, 6 ET 12.

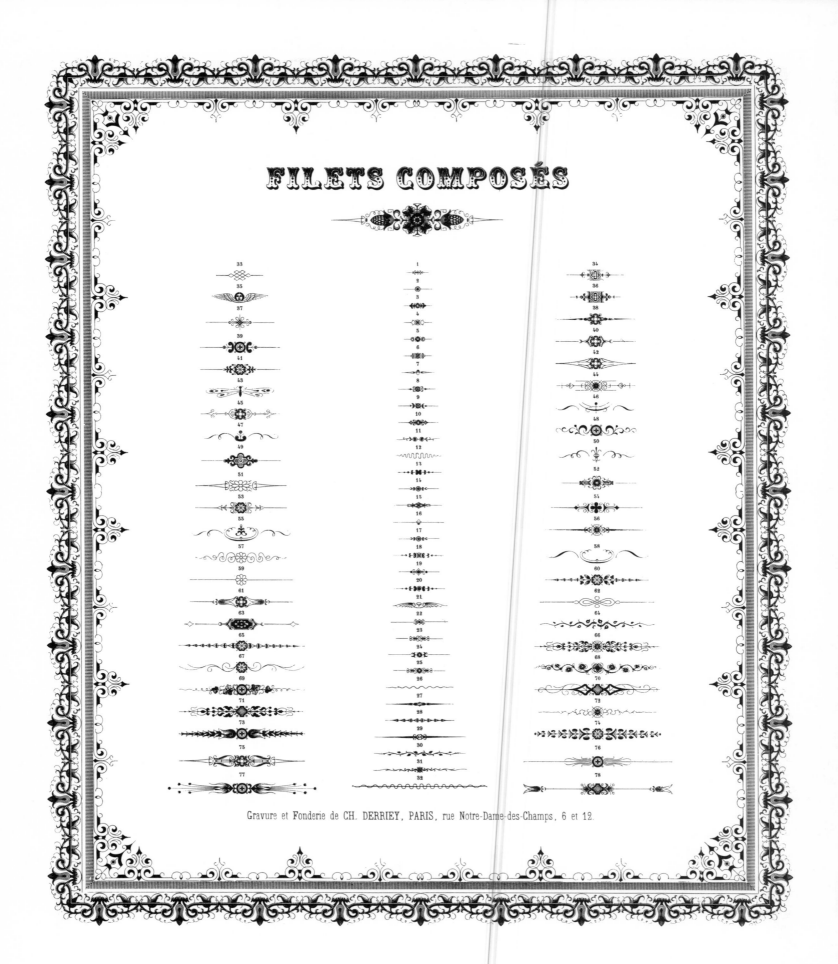

# FILETS COMPOSÉS

Gravure et Fonderie de CH. DERRIEY, PARIS, rue Notre-Dame-des-Champs, 6 et 12.

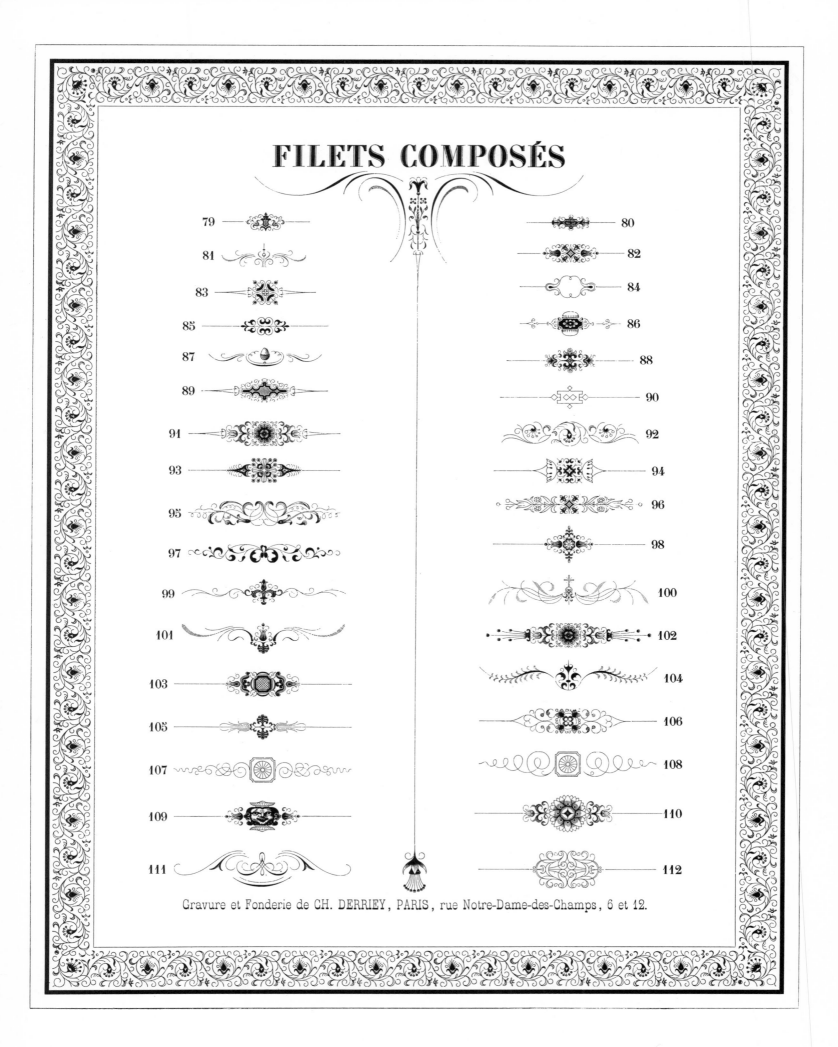

# FILETS COMPOSÉS

79 80
81 82
83 84
85 86
87 88
89 90
91 92
93 94
95 96
97 98
99 100
101 102
103 104
105 106
107 108
109 110
111 112

Gravure et Fonderie de CH. DERRIEY, PARIS, rue Notre-Dame-des-Champs, 6 et 12.

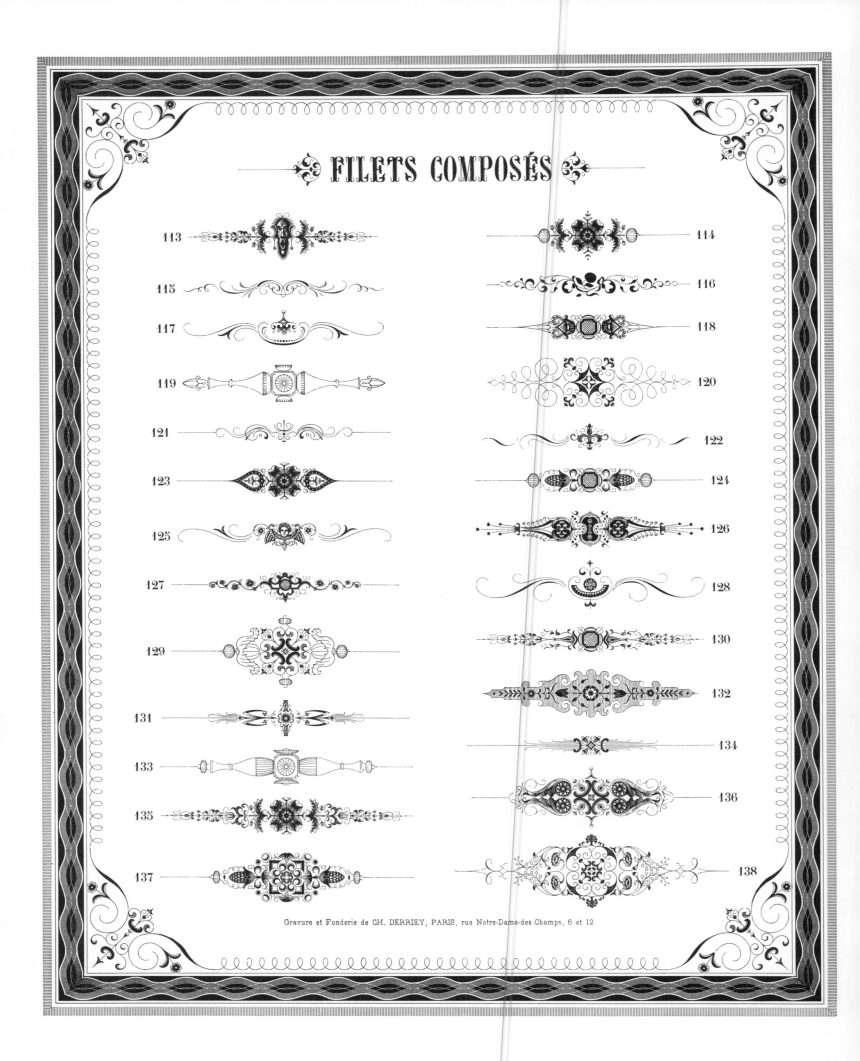

FILETS COMPOSÉS

113

114

115

116

117

118

119

120

121

122

123

124

125

126

127

128

129

130

131

132

133

134

135

136

137

138

Gravure et Fonderie de CH. DERRIEY, PARIS, rue Notre-Dame-des-Champs, 6 et 12

# ❦ FILETS EN LAMES ❦

| | |
|---|---|
| **Corps 1.** | **Corps 5.** |
| 1 | 33 |
| 2 | 34 |
| **Corps 2.** | 35 |
| 3 | 36 |
| 4 | 37 |
| 5 | 38 |
| 6 | 39 |
| **Corps 3.** | 40 |
| 7 | 41 |
| 8 | 42 |
| 9 | 43 |
| 10 | 44 |
| 11 | 45 |
| 12 | 46 |
| 13 | 47 |
| 14 | 48 |
| **Corps 4.** | 49 |
| 15 | 50 |
| 16 | 51 |
| 17 | **Corps 6.** |
| 18 | 52 |
| 19 | 53 |
| 20 | 54 |
| 21 | 55 |
| 22 | 56 |
| 23 | 57 |
| 24 | 58 |
| 25 | 59 |
| 26 | 60 |
| **Corps 5.** | 61 |
| 27 | |
| 28 | |
| 29 | |
| 30 | |
| 31 | |
| 32 | |

Gravure et Fonderie de CH. DERRIEY, PARIS, rue Notre-Dame-des-Champs, 6 et 12.

# FILETS EN LAMES

Corps 8.

62

63

64

65

66

67

68

69

70

71

72

73

74

75

Corps 10.

76

77

78

79

80

81

82

83

84

85

86

Corps 10.

87

88

89

90

91

92

93

94

95

96

97

98

99

100

101

102

103

104

105

106

107

Corps 12

108

109

Gravure et Fonderie de CH. DERRIEY, PARIS, rue Notre-Dame-des-Champs, 6 et 12.

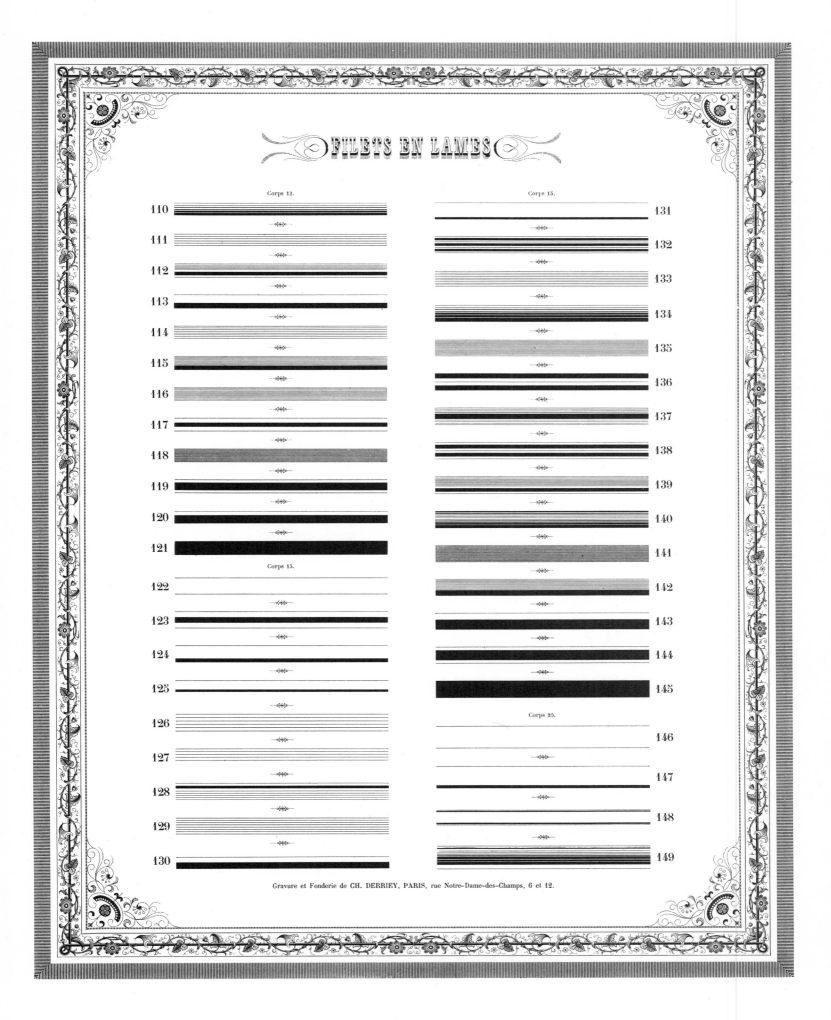

FILETS EN LAMES

Corps 12.

Corps 13.

Corps 15.

Corps 20.

Gravure et Fonderie de CH. DERRIEY, PARIS, rue Notre-Dame-des-Champs, 6 et 12.

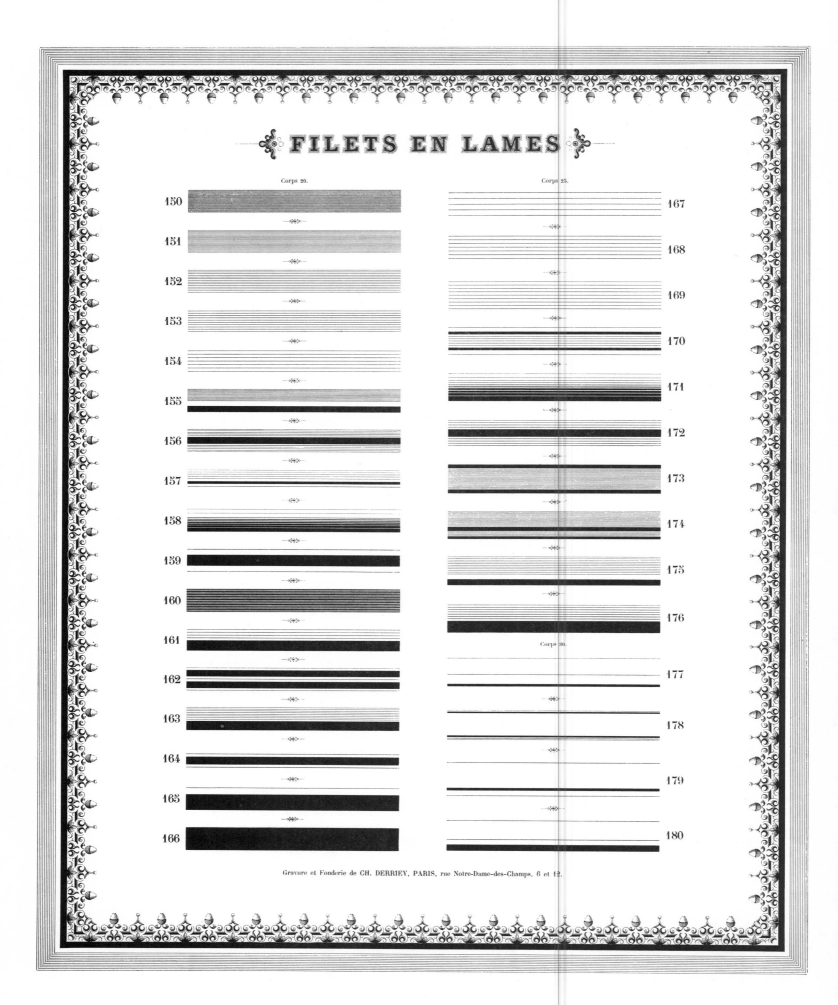

FILETS EN LAMES

Corps 20.

Corps 25.

Corps 30.

Gravure et Fonderie de CH. DERRIEY, PARIS, rue Notre-Dame-des-Champs, 6 et 12.

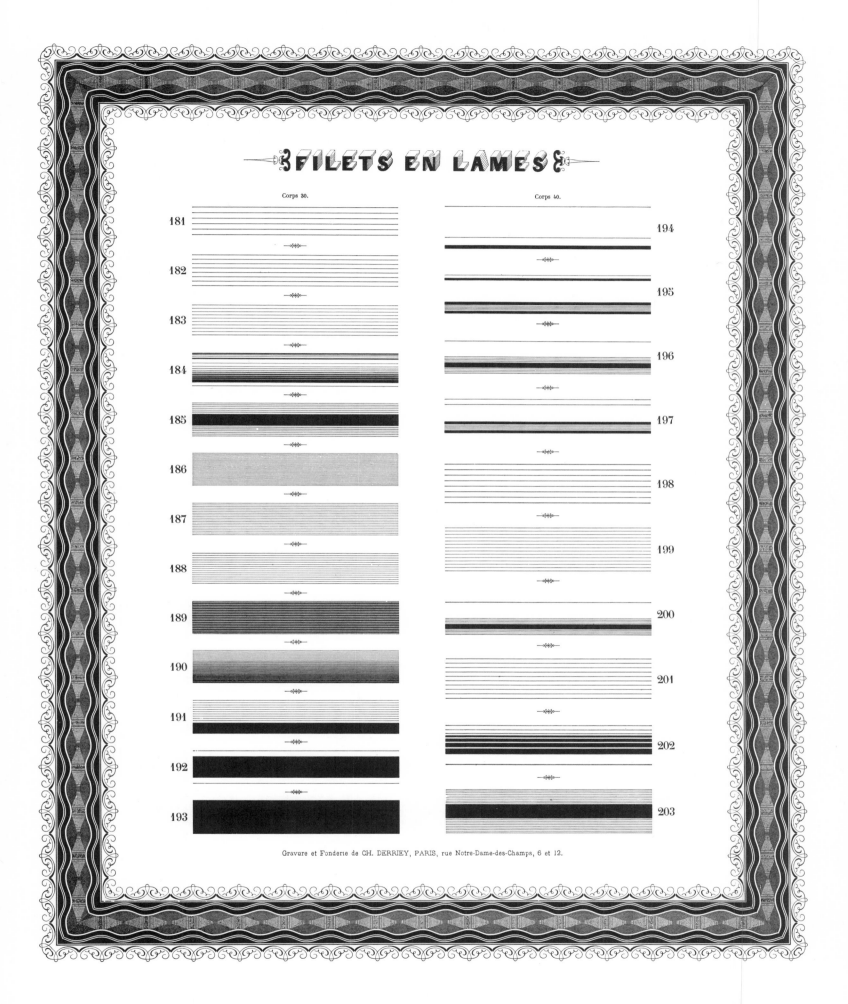

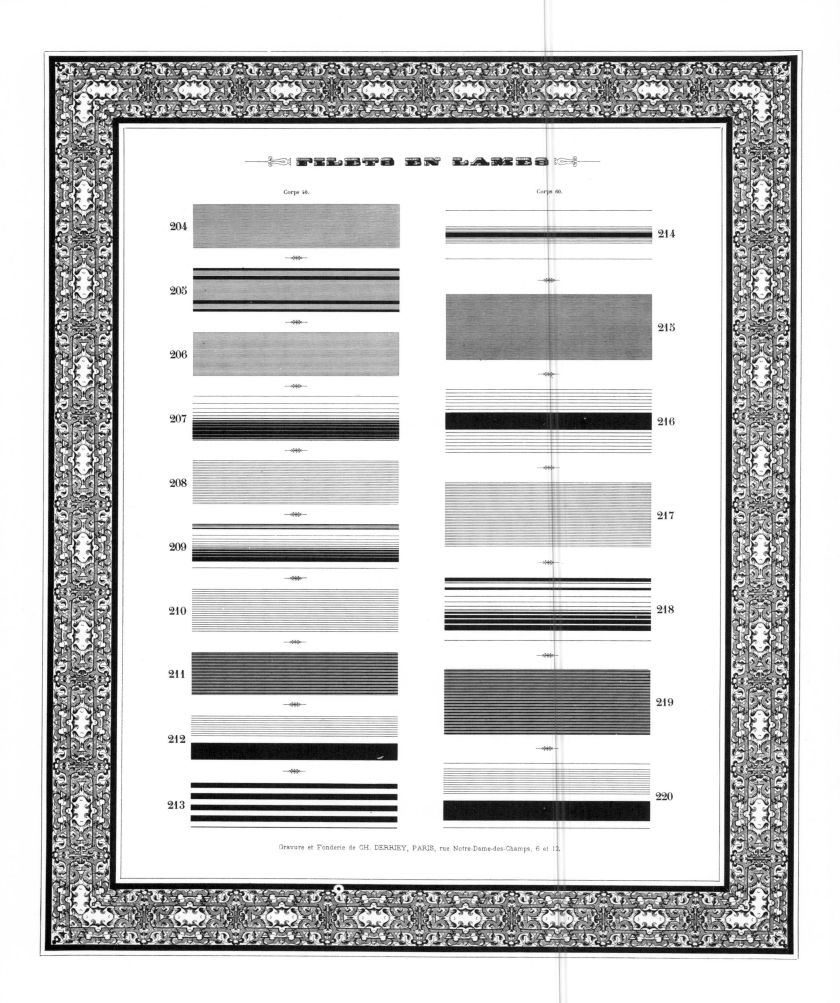

# FILETS EN LAMES

## POINTILLÉS, ONDULÉS & GUILLOCHÉS

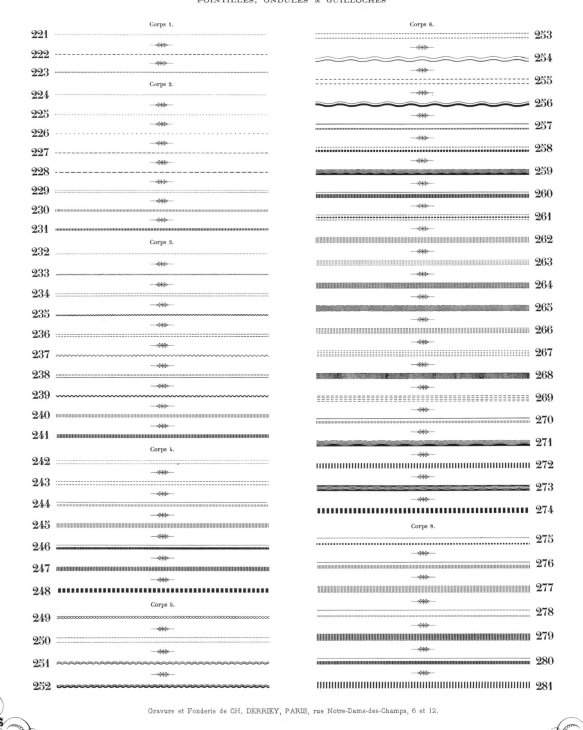

Gravure et Fonderie de CH. DERRIEY, PARIS, rue Notre-Dame-des-Champs, 6 et 12.

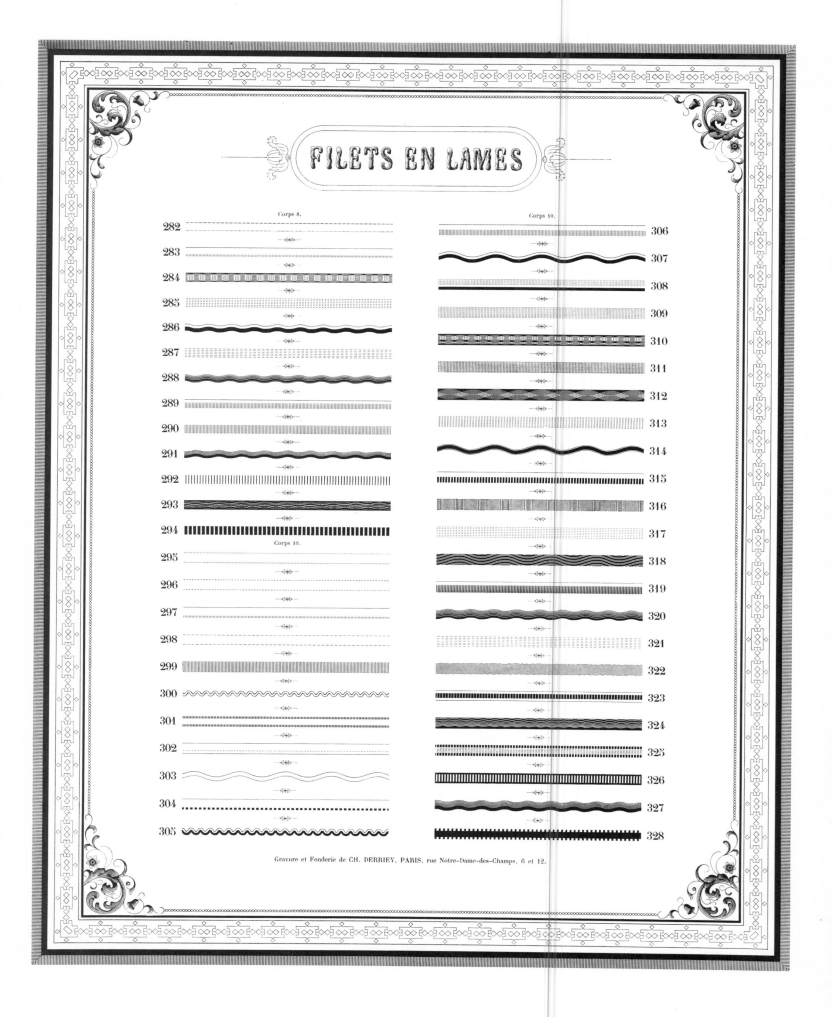

# FILETS EN LAMES

Corps 8.

282
283
284
285
286
287
288
289
290
291
292
293
294

Corps 10.

295
296
297
298
299
300
301
302
303
304
305

Corps 10.

306
307
308
309
310
311
312
313
314
315
316
317
318
319
320
321
322
323
324
325
326
327
328

Gravure et Fonderie de CH. DERRIEY, PARIS, rue Notre-Dame-des-Champs, 6 et 12.

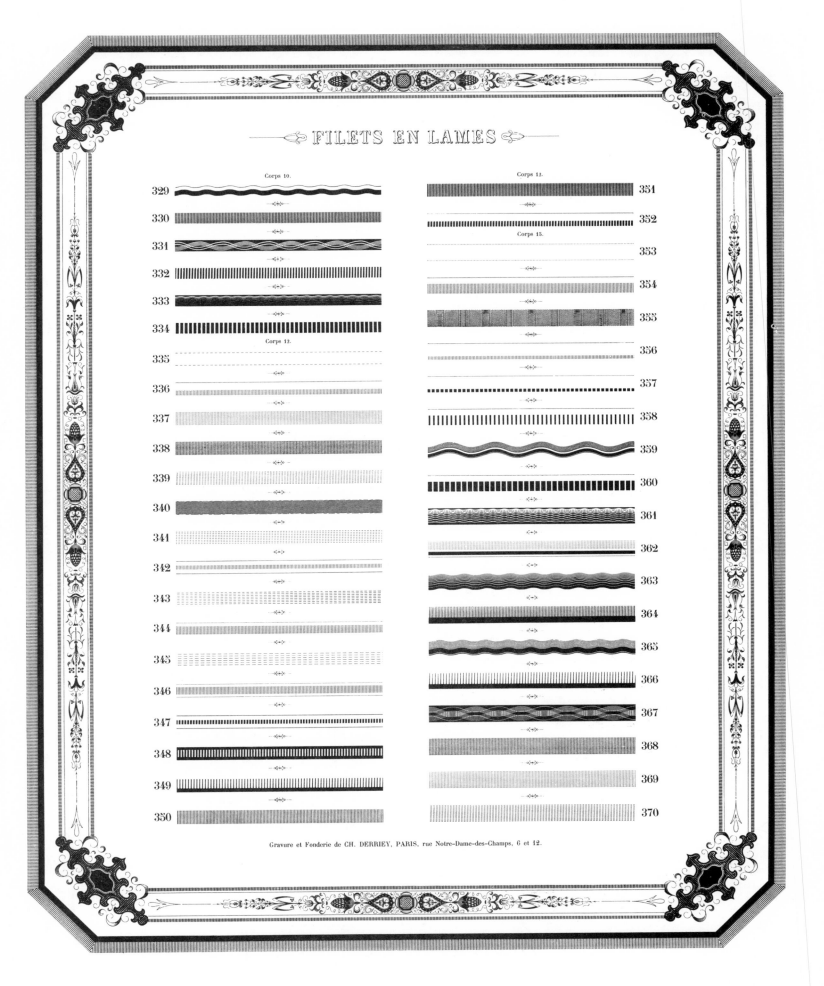

FILETS EN LAMES

Gravure et Fonderie de CH. DERRIEY, PARIS, rue Notre-Dame-des-Champs, 6 et 12.

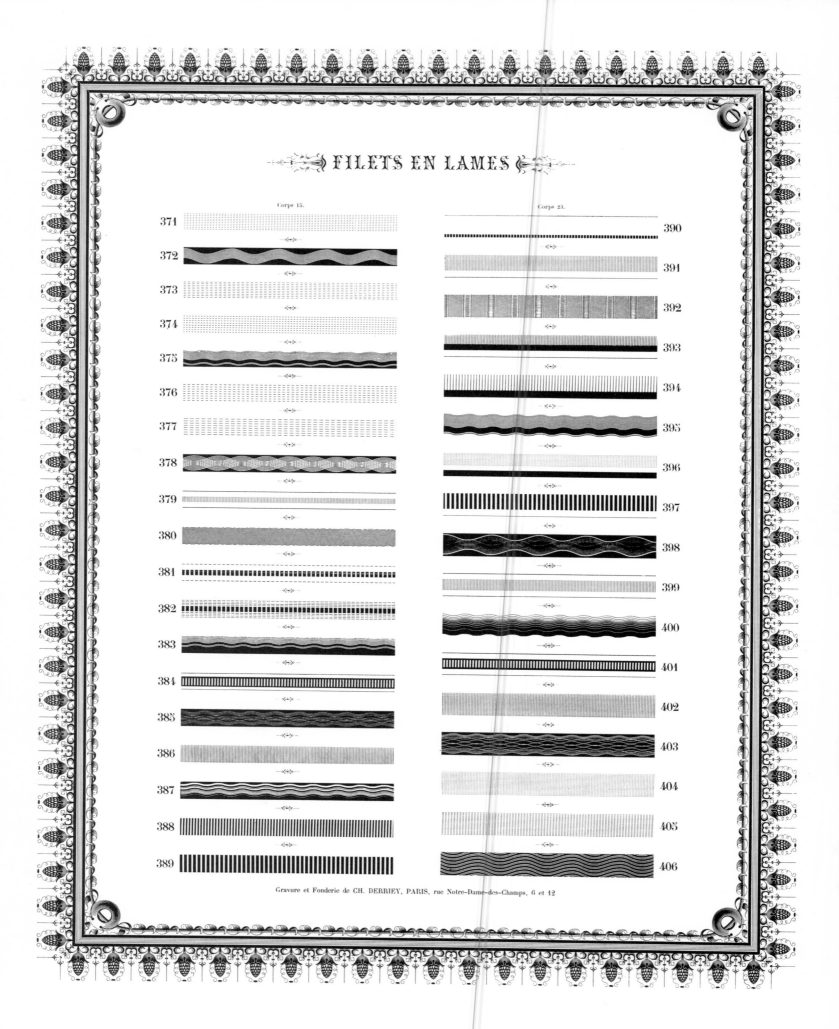

FILETS EN LAMES

Corps 15.

Corps 25.

Gravure et Fonderie de CH. DERRIEY, PARIS, rue Notre-Dame-des-Champs, 6 et 12

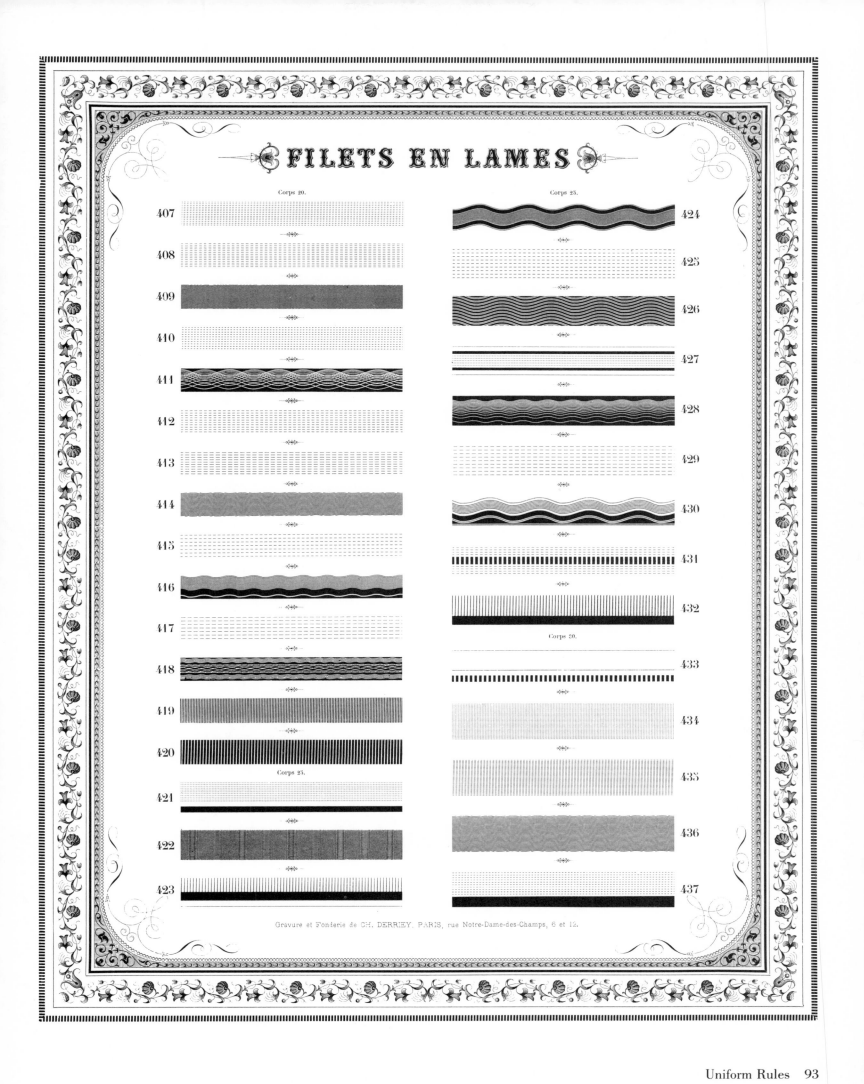

FILETS EN LAMES

Corps 20.

Corps 25.

407

424

408

425

409

426

410

427

411

428

412

429

413

430

414

431

415

432

416

Corps 20.

417

433

418

419

434

420

435

Corps 25.

421

436

422

437

423

Gravure et Fonderie de CH. DERRIEY, PARIS, rue Notre-Dame-des-Champs, 6 et 12.

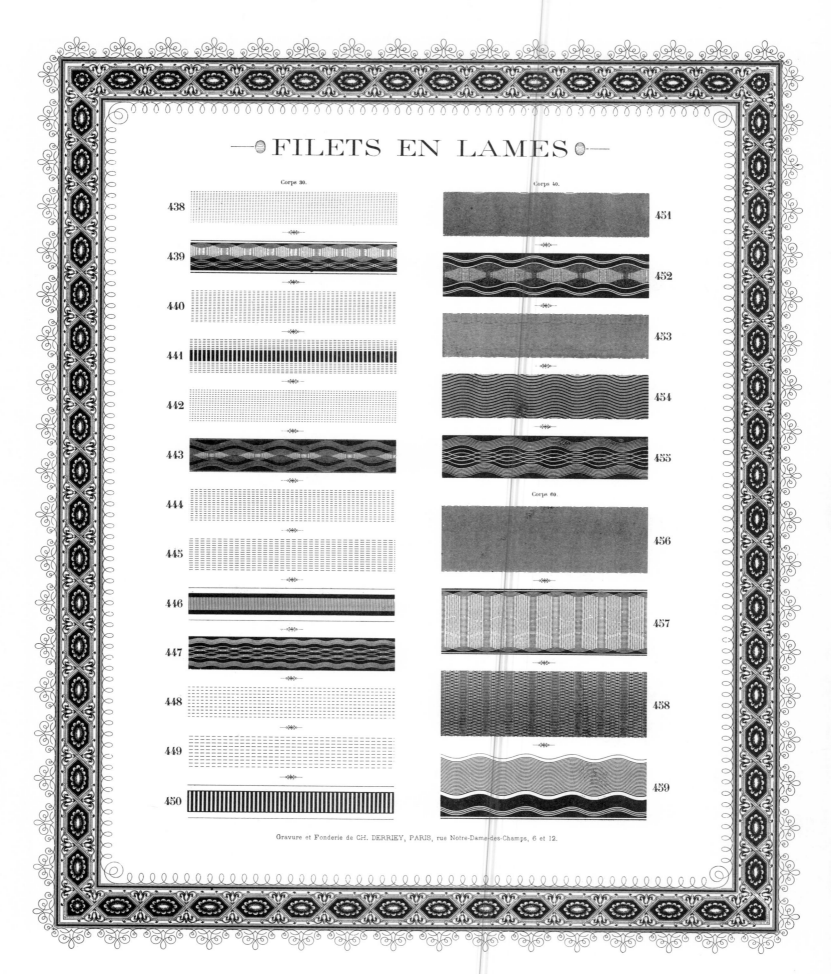

# FILETS EN LAMES

Corps 30.

Corps 40.

Corps 60.

Gravure et Fonderie de CH. DERRIEY, PARIS, rue Notre-Dame-des-Champs, 6 et 12.

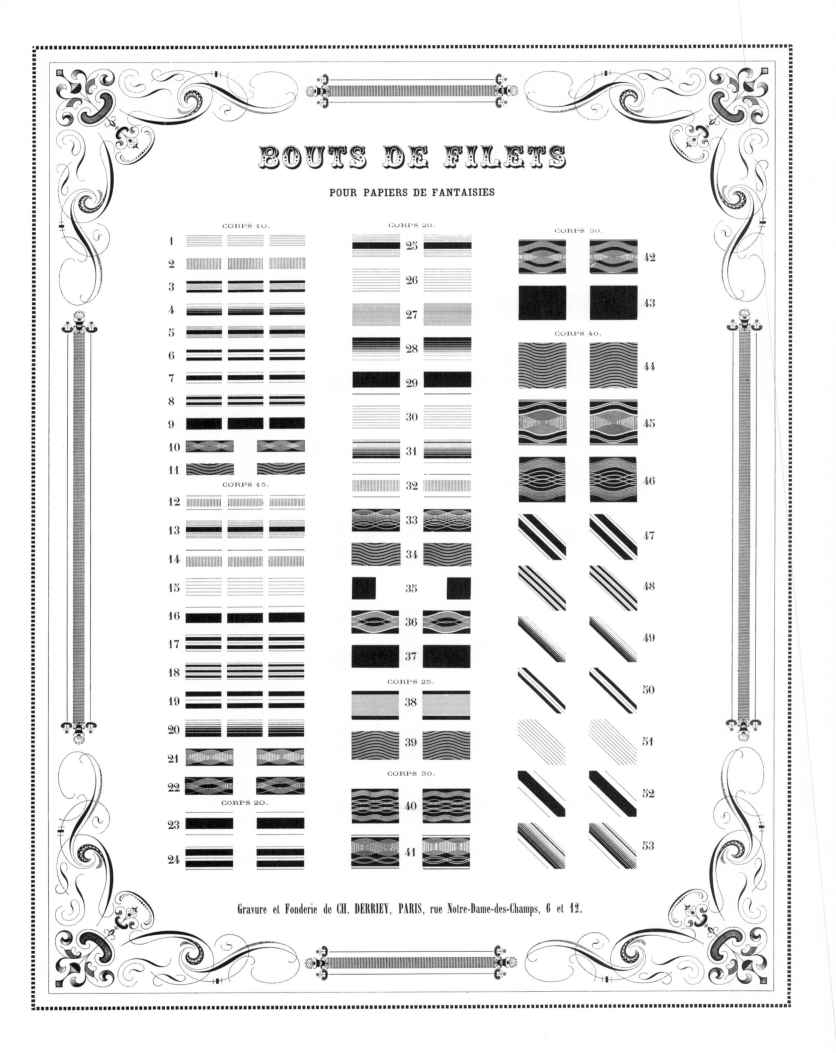

# BOUTS DE FILETS

## POUR PAPIERS DE FANTAISIES

Gravure et Fonderie de CH. DERRIEY, PARIS, rue Notre-Dame-des-Champs, 6 et 12.

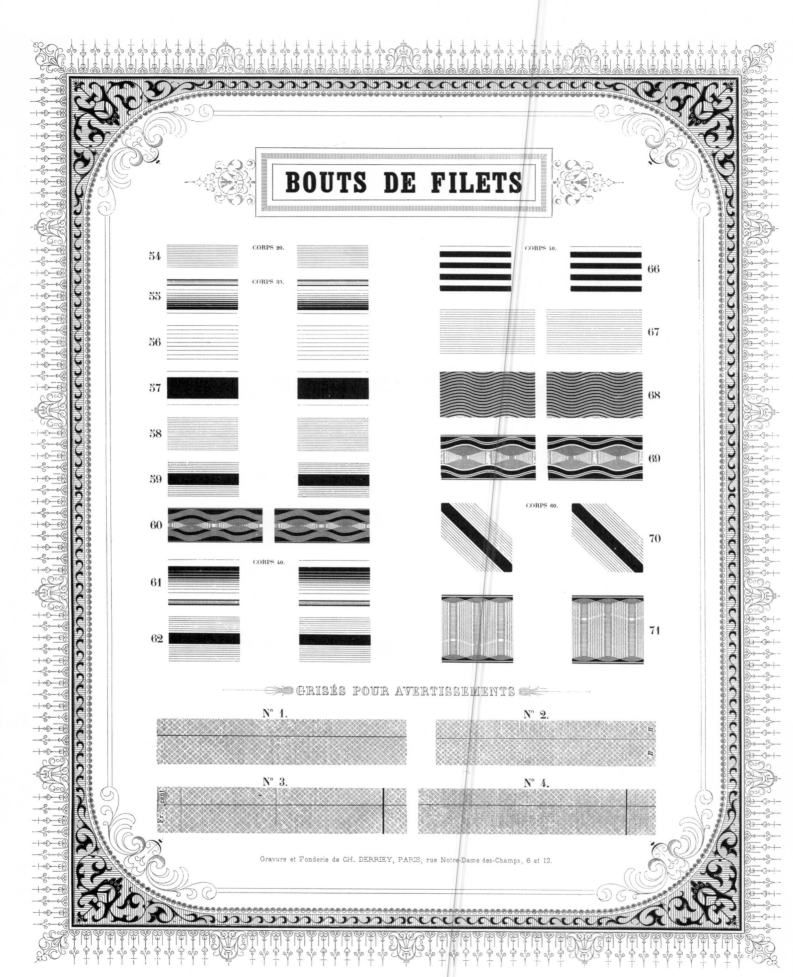

# BOUTS DE FILETS

GRISÉS POUR AVERTISSEMENTS

Gravure et Fonderie de CH. DERRIEY, PARIS, rue Notre-Dame-des-Champs, 6 et 12.

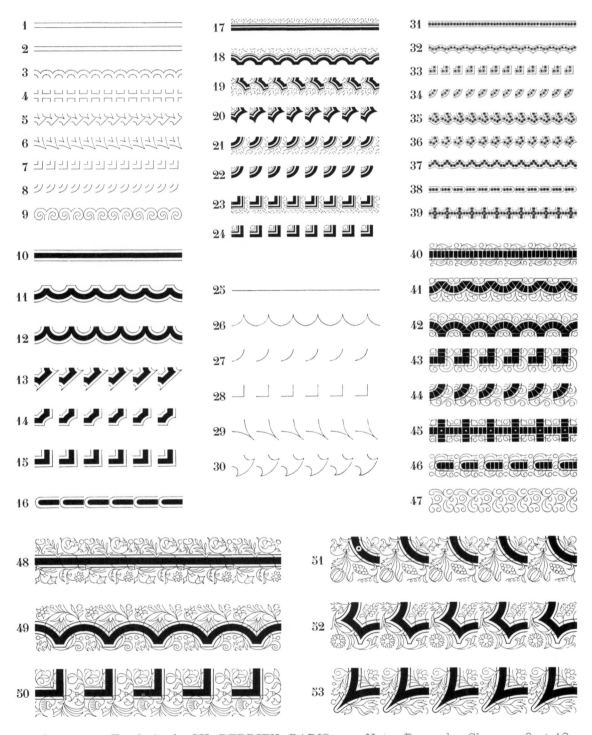

# FILETS MOBILES

Gravure et Fonderie de CH. DERRIEY, PARIS, rue Notre-Dame-des-Champs, 6 et 12.

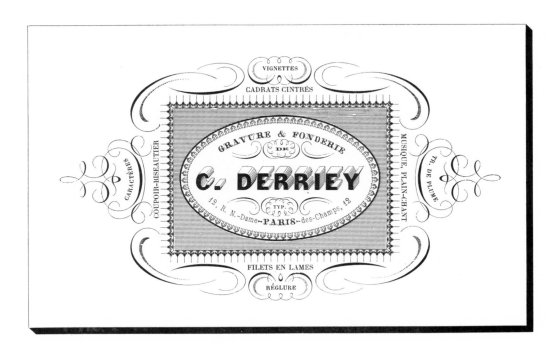

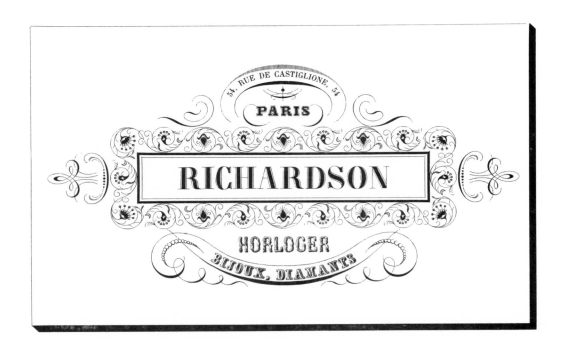

**GRAND HOTEL DU CHEMIN DE FER DU NORD**

TENU PAR GRÉGOIRE

TABLE-D'HOTE
confortable
Déjeûner à 3 francs
Dìner à 5 francs
RESTAURANT
à la Carte

APPARTEMENTS
complets
Chambres de 3 à 8 fr.
Salons de 4 à 10 fr.
BAINS
dans le Jardin

**PARIS**

*RUE DE RIVOLI, 48*

LE 25 AOUT 1859, A MINUIT

JARDIN MABILLE

**BAL DE NUIT**

PRIX : 20 FRANCS

SOUPER , RAFRAICHISSEMENTS

Gravure et Fonderie de CH. DERRIEY, PARIS, rue Notre-Dame-des-Champs, 6 et 12.

INSTITUT IMPÉRIAL DE FRANCE

SÉANCE PUBLIQUE

Le 5 Avril 1860, Réception de Monsieur

ALEXANDRE DUMAS

Comme Membre de l'Académie Française

Porte **B**

Cette Carte est Personnelle

Escalier **C**

CHEMIN DE FER DU NORD

A 3 heures de relevée, à la Gare, clos St-Lazare

Assemblée Générale du 4 Mai 1860

NUMÉRO            CARTE D'ADMISSION            VOIX

Reçu de M _____

Actions au Porteur qui lui seront rendues contre le présent.

Le Caissier de la Compagnie,

Gravure et Fonderie de CH. DERRIEY, PARIS, rue Notre-Dame-des-Champs, 6 et 12.

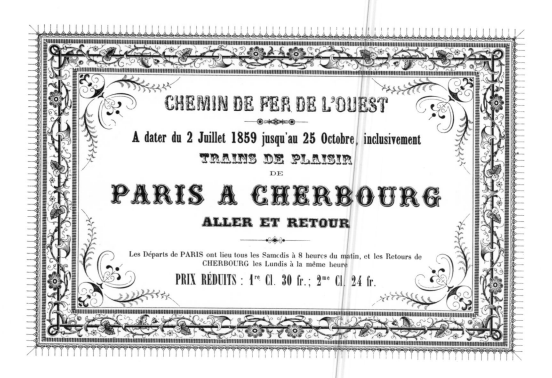

Gravure et Fonderie de CH. DERRIEY. PARIS, rue Notre-Dame-des-Champs, 6 et 12.

Gravure et Fonderie de CH. DERRIEY, PARIS, rue Notre-Dame-des-Champs, 6 et 12.

*Paris, le* _____ *186*

**PRÉFECTURE**
**DU**
**DÉPARTEMENT DE LA SEINE**

## Le Sénateur Préfet de la Seine

*a M* _____

_____

_____

_____

## Société d'Encouragement

**POUR**

**L'INDUSTRIE NATIONALE**

*Reconnue comme Établissement d'utilité publique par Ordonnance Royale du 21 Avril 1824*

**RUE BONAPARTE, 44**

*Paris, le* _____ *196*

*M* _____

_____

_____

_____

Gravure et Fonderie de CH. DERRIEY, PARIS, rue Notre-Dame-des-Champs, 6 et 12.

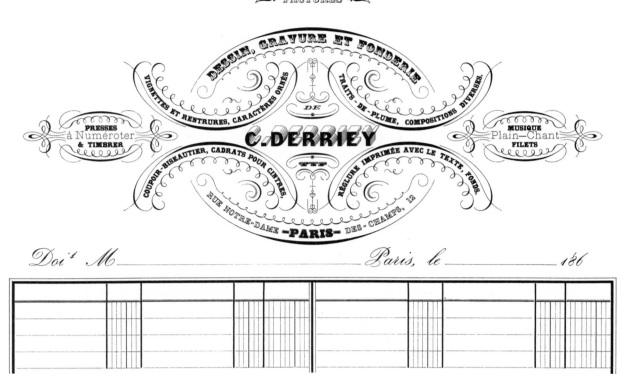

**DESSIN, GRAVURE ET FONDERIE**

VIGNETTES ET RENTRURES, CARACTÈRES ORNÉS.
TRAITS-DE-PLUME, COMPOSITIONS DIVERSES.

*DE*

**C. DERRIEY**

COUPOIR-BISEAUTIER, CADRATS POUR CINTRES.
RÉGLURE IMPRIMÉE AVEC LE TEXTE, FONDS.

PRESSES
à Numéroter
& TIMBRER

MUSIQUE
Plain—Chant
FILETS

RUE NOTRE-DAME -PARIS- DES-CHAMPS, 12

*Doit M_____ Paris, le _____ 186*

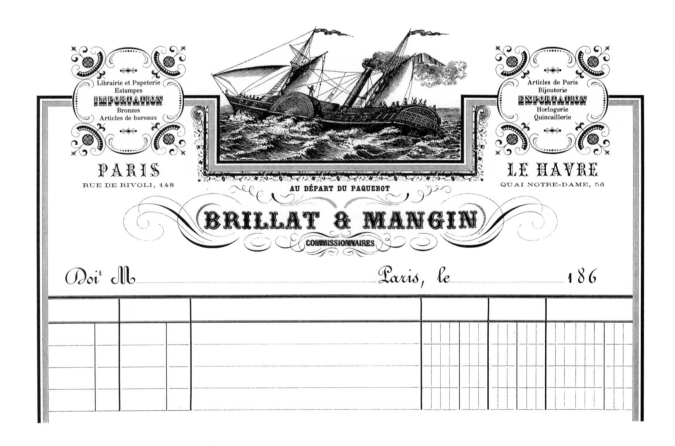

Librairie et Papeterie
Estampes
**IMPORTATION**
Bronzes
Articles de bureaux

Articles de Paris
Bijouterie
**EXPORTATION**
Horlogerie
Quincaillerie

**PARIS**
RUE DE RIVOLI, 148

AU DÉPART DU PAQUEBOT

**LE HAVRE**
QUAI NOTRE-DAME, 56

**BRILLAT & MANGIN**

COMMISSIONNAIRES

*Doit M_____ Paris, le _____ 186*

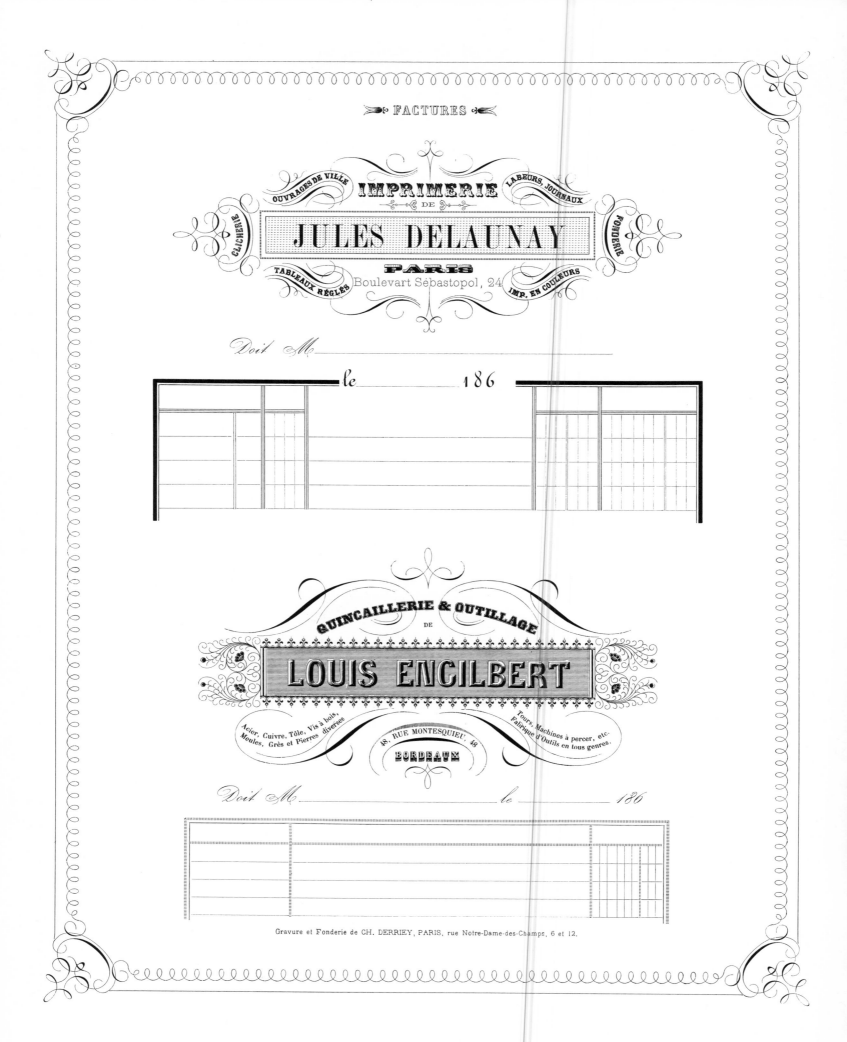

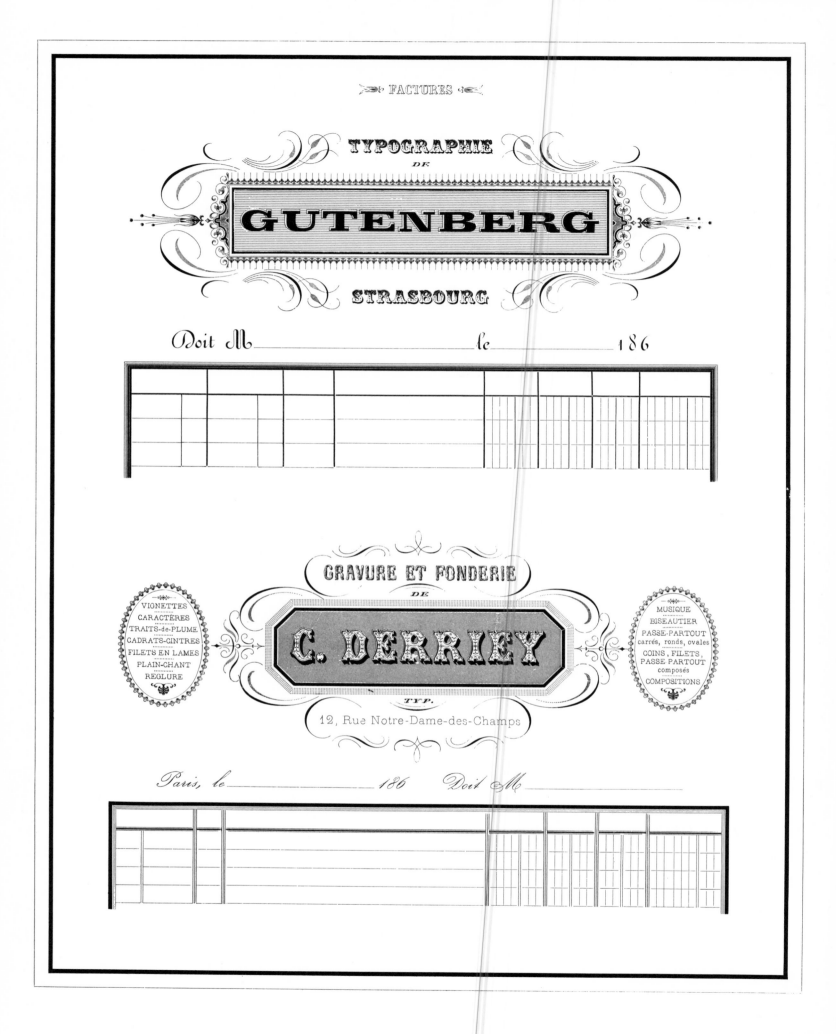

**BOIS DE MENUISERIE**

DE

**CHARPENTIER**

Sapin du Nord et de France, Noyer

QUAI DE LA RAPÉE, 46

PARIS

Chêne, Hêtre, Scierie mécanique

*Livré à M_____ le _____ 186_*

**FONDERIE DE CUIVRE**

DE

**MARTINEAU**

À

PARIS

15, Rue Ménilmontant, 15

NAPOLÉON III EMPEREUR

*Livré le _____ 186_ à M_____*

Gravure et Fonderie de CH. DERRIEY, PARIS, rue Notre-Dame-des-Champs, 6 et 12

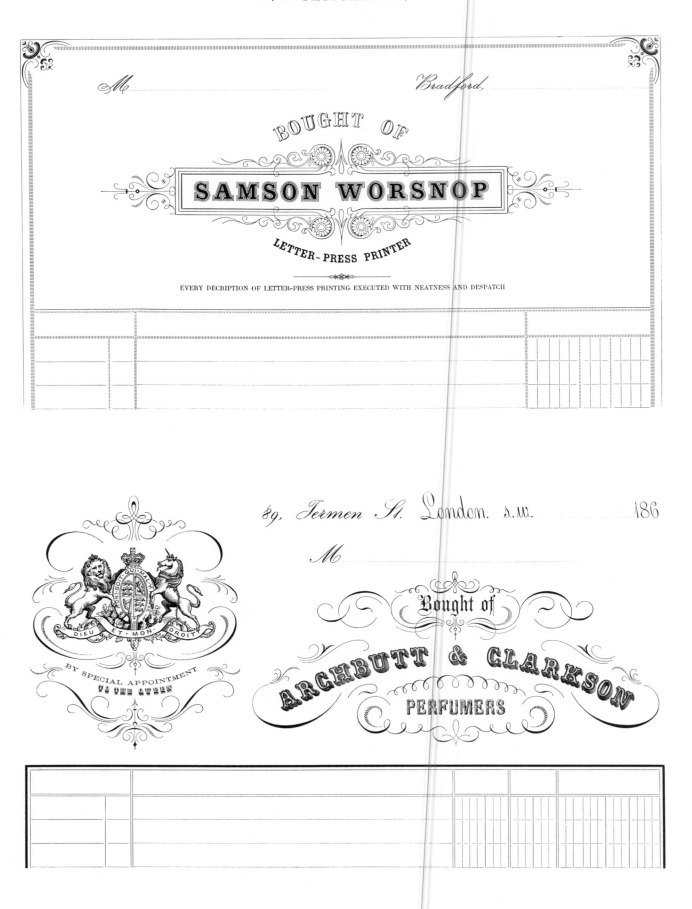

BOUGHT OF

SAMSON WORSNOP

LETTER-PRESS PRINTER

EVERY DECRIPTION OF LETTER-PRESS PRINTING EXECUTED WITH NEATNESS AND DESPATCH

89, Jermen St. London. S.W.        186

Bought of

ARCHBUTT & CLARKSON

PERFUMERS

DIEU · ET · MON · DROIT

BY SPECIAL APPOINTMENT TO THE QUEEN

Gravure et Fonderie de CH. DERRIEY, PARIS, rue Notre-Dame-des-Champs, 6 et 12.

CONTES
DE
PERRAULT

ILLUSTRÉS PAR

GUSTAVE DORÉ

H

PARIS

CHEZ HETZEL, ÉDITEUR LIBRAIRE
rue Jacob, 18

Gravure et Fonderie de CH. DERRIEY, PARIS, rue Notre-Dame-des-Champs, 6 et 12.

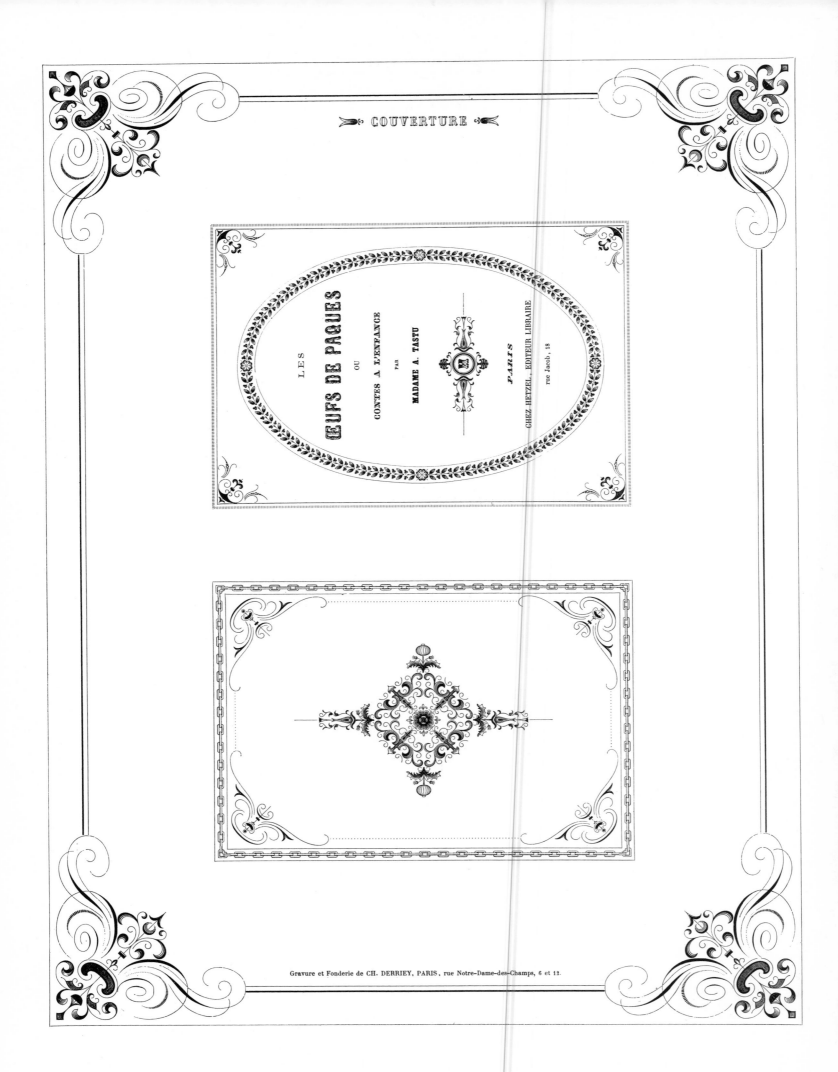

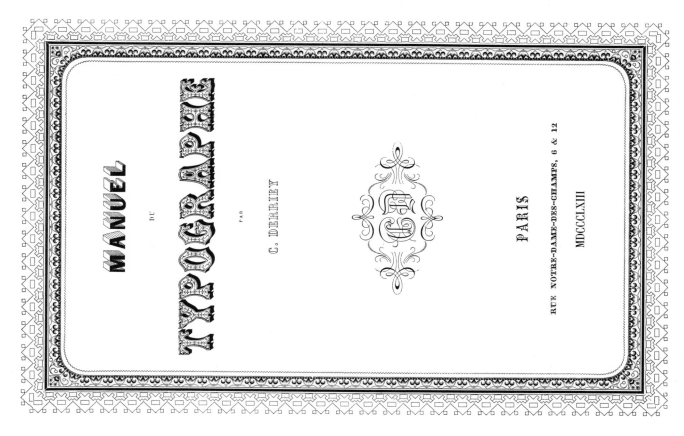

**MANUEL**

DU

**TYPOGRAPHE**

PAR

C. DERRIEY

**PARIS**

RUE NOTRE-DAME-DES-CHAMPS, 6 & 12

MDCCCLXIII

➤• TITRE & COUVERTURE •◄